Racism, Sexism, Trumpism,
Pseudo-Christianity
and the Cinema

Racism, Sexism, Trumpism, Pseudo-Christianity and the Cinema

LIONEL BARRY HARRIS

ReadersMagnet, LLC

Racism, Sexism, Trumpism, Pseudo-Christianity and the Cinema
Copyright © 2020 by Lionel Barry Harris

Published in the United States of America
ISBN Paperback: 978-1-952896-42-2
ISBN eBook: 978-1-952896-43-9

This book is written to provide information and motivation to readers. Its purpose is not to render any type of psychological, legal, or professional advice of any kind. The content is the sole opinion and expression of the author, and not necessarily that of the publisher.

All rights reserved. No part of this publication may be reproduced, stored in a retrieval system or transmitted in any way by any means, electronic, mechanical, photocopy, recording or otherwise without the prior permission of the author except as provided by USA copyright law.

ReadersMagnet, LLC
10620 Treena Street, Suite 230 | San Diego, California, 92131 USA
1.619.354.2643 | www.readersmagnet.com

Book design copyright © 2020 by ReadersMagnet, LLC. All rights reserved.
Cover design by Ericka Obando
Interior design by Shemaryl Tampus

Contents

About the Author vii

Prologue ix

Racism 1

Sexism 64

Trumpism 88

Pseudo Christianity 110

Epilogue 147

IN LOVING MEMORY OF—
My wife – "GLORIA"
My mother – "RUBY"
My uncle – "BILL"
My brother – "GARY"
My brother – "TARAN"
&
My dear friend—
'DORIS JOHNSON'
I dearly miss each and
every one of them and
thank God for crossing
our paths!

About the Author

LIONEL, BARRY HARRIS is a native of the city of Saint Louis, Missouri. After serving a three-year tour in the United States Army, he persistently pursued his writing desires while, simultaneously, engaging in a whole gamut of diverse and interesting jobs. Along with managing a large janitorial service (at the age of twenty-two), he was subsequently employed by the federal government–the Saint Louis Police Department, the Wagner Electric Company, the Potter Electric Company, and (most gratifying and enduring of them all) the Saint Louis public schools at the high school level. In addition to the foregoing, Harris worked part-time in the GED educational program, served as a department store salesman, drove a school bus for the Ferguson Florissant School District (six years), and currently drives a courtesy bus for senior citizens in Saint Louis county. Although HARRIS recently penned "Racism, Sexism, Trumpism and Pseudo-Christianity," he authored "Dark Yesterdays–Bright Tomorrows," "The Long and Winding Road" and "On the Wings of Tragedy."

Prologue

Although they are at times elusive, sometimes soundly asleep and practically languishing on life-support occasionally, I continue to believe that here in the 21st century, even amidst the calamity and controversy of the Donald Trump presidency, that two age-old principles known as truth and righteousness are still relevant and still very much afoot. They are, however, under daily and steady assault and their enemies are, both, relentless and plentiful. But despite the onslaught's ferocity and resolve, I cannot bring myself to believe that total submission and victory is eminent. As long as individuals with integrity and fortitude continue to "thirst for righteousness" and "fight the good fight," blatant evil will not emerge triumphant. And make no mistake about it, unadulterated evil is not only on the front line with the opposing forces, it is boldly leading the charge. And take note of this also: Even if you're not an avid fan of God per se, just stay focused and ever-watchful, and you will come to realize that there is such a being as Satan. And in spite of lurking in the shadows, he is the chief orchestrator of this particular war and all other wars to come.

Now, some people may brand me an alarmist and they may very well call me melodramatic too; my even suggesting that we are in some sort of war, but those critics would be wrong on both counts. Evil forces are able to secure the high ground in any battle because they are ultra-serious and united in their assault and we, as the opposition, simply are not. Naive as it sounds, the greater majority of us think if we exercise patience, assert moderate resistance and even pray in silence, that right will alternately prevail.

But let's face it. Although "good soundly defeating evil" may be an ever-popular theme in storybooks and a slew of movies, it is seldom applicable to contemporary life and especially when we focus on the United States of America.

I am certain I'm stepping on sensitive toes here (and so be it) but when our country has school-age children killing and maiming fellow classmates, daily inner-city gun violence, grown men behaving like sex-crazed barbarians, racist and home spun terrorists running amok and a power-hungry president who longs to be a king or dictator, and a horde of men who apparently covets the wild west era, there is not a happy ending waiting in the wings. Neither do we see an all-conquering hero riding off into the sunset.

Therefore, it is incumbent upon us (individuals who are not wearing blinders and are not in denial) to step forward and boldly write that elusive happy ending. Or, ideally, you may even emerge as that alluded to hero who saves the day. However, before you bask in accolades and ride off in glory, I suggest that you take a long and in-depth look at yourself. Because if you are an individual who selectively accesses truth and righteousness, then the applause will be muffled and short-lived. To speak bluntly, you'll be reeking with hypocrisy and will be no different than the average, everyday offender. There lies the crux of the problem we are facing today, the authentic reason America is so divided and in a state of chaos and turmoil. Far too many of us have come to believe that such principles as righteousness, truth and even justice are flexible and moldable and, therefore, highly susceptible to revision at a person's every whim.

However, that is not the case. Right is right and wrong is wrong. And no matter how you slice it and no matter how you slant or try to disguise it, it will always be that way. A single person or an entire multitude of people might be skilled at concocting or presenting an alternative "right" but it will not stand in the long run. When Dr. Martin Luther King Jr. declared that, "Truth crushed to earth will rise again," he was talking about righteousness

Racism, Sexism, Trumpism, Pseudo-Christianity and the Cinema

as well. For they are interlocked and are the age-old foundation for, yet, another beleaguered principle known at justice. It, too, cannot justly be modified or reinvented either.

Tragically, the fore stated is where we, as a country, are today. Whether we reflect on RACISM, SEXISM, TRUMPISM or PSEUDO-CHRISTIANITY (Which are the four topics applicable to this book), they are sustained and actively fueled by misrepresentation, subversion, stonewalling and out-and-out lies and if we fail to take decisive measures to halt or derail this runaway train, the impending crash will be catastrophic and long-enduring. And when I say "We," I am not referring to members of Congress (whether they be Republicans, Democrats or Independents), or the various courts, nor law enforcement officials, or men and women of great wealth and fame, and not even clergymen. Unfortunately, so many of the aforementioned are part of the overall problem, and not remotely the solution. Instead, I'm reaching out to the common person here, individuals who are non-partisan and decent, those who are endowed with integrity and an embedded sense of fairness and surely not men and women with self-serving agendas. And I am especially singling out America's fathers and mothers, parents who are charged with teaching their children the tenets of righteousness and honor. That specified group cannot or, at least, should not stand by idle while their offsprings watch America go to hell in a hand-basket.

And that is where we are rapidly headed if we, as loving parents, fail to reaffirm ourselves as beacons of light in our children's lives. Even if we stand guilty of fading into the wood work along the way (and some of us have), it is high-time for us to dust ourselves off and resurface. We owe that resurgence to our children, the neighboring children, to future generations and to ourselves.

Now, you as a reader of this narrative, may brand me accusatory and/or judgmental. And, maybe, you're right. You may even resent my tone and abrupt manner. And to a certain degree, I apologize for that. However, in regards to individuals who might angrily ask, "Who the hell are you?" or even, "Who the hell do you think you are?" I feel obliged to address your queries. I will do it with humility and marked honesty. First and foremost, I am a proud 74-year-old black man who was born and bred in the U.S. of A. And when I reflect upon the adage "With age comes wisdom," I automatically think of myself. But my feelings are neither due to haughtiness nor arrogance, it is, instead, based on my personal relationships with an array of special individuals who adorned my life along the way. Since many of them were thirty years my senior, in a benevolent sense I was thinking like a seasoned elderly person when I was but a young, inquisitive man. And that's a heartfelt tribute to my elderly mentors, not to me.

With the foregoing stated, I suppose in the eyesight of some readers I'm a perennial nobody; not that that offends me or remotely resonates with me. Admittedly, I have no heralded claim to fame, no impressive initials trailing my name and no accumulated wealth or riches that, to some folks, catapults one select person above the average, everyday American citizen. But what I do have, and I sincerely wish it was commonplace and contagious as well, is an insatiable affection for unvarnished truth and basic justice. And at this juncture in my rather long life, those two dual-headed qualities are M.I.A. (missing in action) and practically extinct. Even a perennial "nobody" could credibly argue and belabor that point.

So, please try and think of me as a sober voice of reason. It really doesn't matter that I worked with teenagers for 40 years, or that I was married for almost three fourths of those years and managed to raise three children. Or that I served a stint in the U.S. army and grew up in urban Saint Louis with four brothers, a staple mother and an errant father. And while it is all quite true and greatly influenced my entire being, the forestated does not completely define me. And I'm compelled to add the following: We are, after all, in America and, therefore, neither does my black skin define me and render my views irrelevant and void.

I imagine some people at this juncture, especially white people,

Racism, Sexism, Trumpism, Pseudo-Christianity and the Cinema

will accuse me of throwing them a vicious curve. A few of them might even charge me with "playing the race card," I suppose. But let me give you my personal assessment on that. I have played various card games since I was six (6) years old (a very long time), and I honestly do not know which card in a standard deck is the frequently-touted "race card." I'm not positive, but it might be one of the jokers because when people engage in most card competitions–the two jokers are both left in the original card box. I am not saying that the charge is always unfounded and baseless, I'm simply stating that it never worked for me. Even when I filed a credible grievance with the EEOC (Equal Employment Opportunity Commission) it was fruitless.

Do I have an axe to grind or an ulterior motive? I half-heartedly plead guilty of that. But it's not about some mysterious race card or even an inclination to assign blame to any single group of people. In the final analysis we are all Americans and in spite of religion, nationality and racial differences, we are all adrift on the same enormous ship. However, if we do not come together and openly discuss our hostilities and shortcomings, our course will always be bumpy and hazardous. Furthermore, if we continue to overlook or blot out the obnoxious elephant in the room, which is racism (and many of us are expert in doing so), we will never come close to becoming a nation united. And as the old saying concludes, "A house divided cannot stand." In addition, we must always remember that a ship called the "Titanic" perished in ocean waters. Are we willing, then, to make some tough concessions? To take a hard line and an in-depth view of our own faults and our own frailties? Above all, are we willing to make a concerted effort to change? And if the answer is "yes" to that query (and the dissenters will number in the millions) it will alternately mean that you will openly submit yourself to a novel education and a new awakening also. What I'm suggesting is this: Erroneously, white folks think they know black folks! However, the majority of them are so wrong it's almost shameful. But, on the other hand, we, as black people, do tend to know white folks.

However, it's not because I believe black citizens are smarter or more discerning than our white counterparts. It's simply because black people, as a minority race, have traditionally been exposed to Caucasian history (in fact, I've always substituted the pronoun "his" with "white" in that term) and white folks, as the dominant race, are regularly granted a rather obscure and tainted insight into black lives by simply viewing the daily news broadcasts and seeing numerous violent, ghetto-based movies. Therefore, instead of seeing the real hard-working, law-abiding black citizens (people whom I've known all my life), whites seem fixated on the stereo typical and celluloid versions. And, apparently, that racist mind-set has tremendous staying power. Personally, I think some white folks withdraws some kind of sick refuge from that viewpoint. It heightens their false feeling of superiority.

In reality, that false presumption is a soothing and inspiring comfort to a great number of white people. If they did not have that premise to snuggle up with at nightfall, they could not peacefully fall asleep. In essence, if they did not have the luxury of looking down upon Afro-American people, they would be all out of sorts. As alluded to in a well-known movie I once saw ("Mississippi Burning," to be specific), it was stated, "If you ain't better than a nigger, who is you better than?

The answer to that question, I suspect, is, "It's blowing in the wind" because it is void of innateness, it is not verifiable and it is totally nonsensical. It's a figment of white America's imagination, even when we focus on poor and destitute Caucasians. Just by looking down on Afro-American people (despite the social or monetary status of the observed black folks), they, somehow, feel fortunate and emboldened. In essence, they would rather be poor and downtrodden than to be born with dark skin.

Although I never understood the above mind-set, I thought about it quite a bit. When I was fifteen and in high school, I even

Racism, Sexism, Trumpism, Pseudo-Christianity and the Cinema

asked my social studies teacher if he could provide me insight on the subject. He said I'd be more successful at extracting "blood from a turnip" than trying to understand racism. Said I was trying to derive logic from something that was totally illogical. Then, he made a statement I'll never forget. And, in fact, I've mouthed it time and time again in my life. With a somber face, my teacher declared, "While Caucasians are born into this world with unearned privilege, we, as so-called Negroes, are born with unearned suffering." Then, he added, "Keep that in mind whenever you deal with our people. And don't waste your affection and compassion on white folks, they won't appreciate it."

To be frank, I was neither shocked nor disheartened by my history teacher's sincere and rather bleak assessment regarding race. For I was exposed to white biasness when I was a small child, even before school desegregation began. Honestly, I didn't understand racism then, I didn't understand it when I was a teenager, when I was a soldier in the army, and I don't understand it at present. Even at the age of 74, it is as foreign to me as Outer Mongolia and a bonafide mystery as well.

However, I'm well aware of what my personal problem is. I actually know why I can't comprehend hatred and biasness that, apparently, has no legitimate basis or roots. Aligning myself with the age-old thoughts of my social studies teacher, it's an archaic precept that's illogical, bizarre and absent of common sense! One minute, black people are considered chattel (slaves) and providing free manual labor; and the next minute, they are free men who are frequently lynched, ostracized and systematically annihilated. And that is not only cruel and inhumane, it's downright hypocritical and reeking of insanity! But I'll say this and then leave it alone for the time being: Logically speaking, America's black citizenry should be begrudging and rebellious towards white folks, and not the reverse. Once again I'll admit, I don't understand any of it.

There is something I do know, however. Even upon displacing

comprehension altogether, I know it's not justified, it's contrary to truth and righteousness and it's an ever present pox on this country.

Of course, I am essentially back where I first started. But I've purposely been redundant throughout this piece because I am obsessed with the notion that the long-festering ills of America are treatable and, therefore, not fatal. In spite of my advanced age, and even in the wake of all the ugliness and despair I have personally endured and seen, I am still a die-hard optimist. And I refuse to jump off the simulated ship I alluded to earlier or go down in defeat with it. Not without a sustained and fierce fight!

Hopefully, I am not alone in my aspirations or in my optimism. There has to be people in modern America who are just as passionate and intent about doing the right thing as I am. They are not plentiful, I know that, but they are there. I'm just imploring you, or them, to step up to the proverbial plate. Plainly stated, I'm imploring you (or them) to put your mouth, hopefully, where your heart is.

I realize I'm asking a great deal, especially when it comes to white citizens. Many white individuals are what I call "bad actors." Not because they're phonies, evil or sinister per se but because they are born into their awarded superiority role and delight in leaning into it. They willingly have allowed unearned privilege to take center stage in their lives. Meaning, that although Caucasian babies are oblivious of skin-color while in their mother's womb, they evolve in quick-time and then come to not only embrace the premise, but to bask in it. And, tragically, that's when an inordinate number of white folks elect to cast aside the unearned concept and arrogantly replace it with the selfgradiose term innate (or inborn). And, most significantly, it is at that precise stage when "bad actors" degenerate into low-life "bad apples."

And in case you are unable to differentiate "bad actors" from "bad apples," allow me to give you my take on it. Firstly, it is imperative that you know that bad apples are practically synonymous with "spoiled brats" and millions of people, regardless

Racism, Sexism, Trumpism, Pseudo-Christianity and the Cinema

of their pigmentation or their individual station in life, are keenly aware of the harm and sorrow that permeates from such despicable individuals. Not all of them but from time to time, most of them.

Within this text, I will painstakingly identify them. Many of us personally know them, even if we prefer not to know them. They are the people, who callously justify the near-genocide of Native Americans, the individuals who skirt pass the slavery issue and grieves over the demise of racial segregation and Jim Crow. They are the white-supremacists, the neo-Nazis, the Ku Klux Klan and every other God-awful group who march to the beat of a sick, hate-inspired drummer.

However, even if those select persons are not affiliated with any of the forestated extremist, there's a faction that still clings tight to their "spoiled brat" status. And many of us, as average Americans (and especially the black ones), recognize them also. They're the group who despises the "Black Lives Matter" signs, advocating there should be "White Lives Matter" signs too. They are the faction who resent and demonize the "Dreamers," even though they invoke nightmares in those very same immigrants. And they are the ones who lead the charge for bigger and more rapid-firing rifles and handguns. And if that is not descriptive of a classic and obnoxious spoiled brat, then nothing is. I could even imagine them collectively... declaring, "I am white and I, as a white person, should be granted anything my little heart desires. And furthermore, if you refuse to indulge me (give me the toys I crave), I will throw one of my tantrums." And that, in a nutshell, highlights presumed superiority and unearned privilege at its ugliest and distorted best.

So you see, I have a pretty good understanding of the mentality of America's Caucasian populace, the bad actors and the bad apples as well. Am I contending that there are no "good" actors, no decent and benevolent white people amongst them? Of course, I'm not! Why else would I exert my energy to writing this book? Hopefully, I, can persuade a few white folks and a large segment of minority

xvii

folks also to see the world through my aging and discerning eyes. And although it will be somewhat painful at times (for the reader and myself), sometimes revealing and thought-provoking, at some points; frustrating and hard to believe, and even a bit amusing, it will be the whole truth and nothing but the truth. And that, in itself, is a rarity in today's world.

But as I professed earlier, it will be a tough row to hoe. Because when people are implored to take an in-depth look at the image in their mirror and then are asked to retreat from their secure comfort zone, they are ofttimes resistant and downright combative. However, I'm not remotely shocked or discouraged. As I previously stated, we are actively in the throes of a war.

Once again, I am positive that many folks will strongly denounce me for merely hinting that the assault on truth and righteousness is, in reality, a war. But again, too, I beg to differ with them. War, similar to truth, righteousness and justice is subjective. Therefore, war to me may not be war to another person. But since I'm the advocate here, the old man calling a spade a spade, allow me to further champion my viewpoint.

You see, as a seasoned black man (or Afro-American), I have been privy to a long birds-eye view of our country's state of being. And, sadly, it is chug-full of hypocrisy and absurdity; some of it, outrageous, and some of it, quite laughable. For instance, if our government was as hell-bent on criminalizing and banning America's assault rifles (a clear and present danger) as they are with confiscating and eradicating W.M.D. s in other countries, then the United States, itself, would not be made to resemble a war zone time and time again.

And, probably, because I happen to be a black man also (and a person who has attended the funerals of far too many slain young men and women), my personal take on "Weapons of Mass Destruction" may be strikingly different from others viewpoints too.

For example: If we take a few minutes to revisit that horrendous

Racism, Sexism, Trumpism, Pseudo-Christianity and the Cinema

school shooting that took place in Parkland, Florida on February 14th of this very year, you and I might emerge with diverse takeaways. In fact, I'd venture to bet on it.

Once again, some folks might dismiss me as melodramatic or extreme but when I recall and mourn the 17 victims who died during that 'St. Valentine's Day Massacre,' my thoughts plunge a fathom deeper. Because when you mix in the suffering of the victims who were maimed and wounded on that ominous day, and then empathize with the lament and anguish of that subject Florida community and the nation at large.

When you hone-in on the incredible loss of childhood innocence (those young people will relive that insidious event for the rest of their days.) and then pause and try to imagine the ever-present and widespread grief of those who dearly loved and cherished the deceased victims of that shooting event, you will be hard-pressed to keep your emotions in check.

I know I wasn't able to keep my composure back in February and, honestly, I still struggle with digesting it all. But I must say the following: If the United States of America was not eyewitness to "mass destruction" in mid-February of 2018, then it needs to swiftly remove its blinders and/or purchase a collective pair of bifocals. For it is one thing to be void of insight, but it's an entirely different thing to be absent of empathetic and compassionate eyesight. And that's the truth, the whole truth and–nothing but the truth!

Racism

Until Caucasian people can bring themselves to declare (with sincerity) they would rather be right than be white, the United States of America will always be a sphere of racial hatred, unrest and violence.

Out of the Mouths of Babes

When I was about 8 years old, my 72-year old grand mother voiced a certain comment that, peculiarly, remained with me throughout my life. With a spirit of hope, she stated, "It'll be a whole lot better for the colored folks in this world when the prejudiced white people die out." Of course, as a precocious child I remained silent and did not dare to speak to grandma's statement. (It was 1952 and a kid knew to stay in a child's place in those days). Plus, she wasn't actually talking to me. She was addressing her daughter, my mother.

However, a mere four years later when I was 12, I took the liberty of refreshing Grandma's memory regarding that precise assertion and although she did not readily recall it, I "respectfully" took issue with it anyhow.

Although I wasn't wise enough to know that I was dashing an old woman's hopes, I told Grandma she was squarely wrong. But instead of leaving it at that, I opted to qualify my argument. After all, it was based on a happening that transpired only three days prior and it was fresh on my mind. The following is the essence of the account I presented to her:

During the summer months, and especially when school

was not in session, I frequently worked with my first cousin's husband. His name was Frank and although he regularly worked in construction, he took on a few side jobs to earn extra money. That's where I came in. Under Frank's supervision and laboring for mostly well-to-do Caucasians, I became skilled at detailing newly-built homes, white-washing basements, touch-up interior house painting and cutting and grooming lawns.

I was in the middle of performing the latter task, cutting the front lawn of a large ranch-style home in a suburb called "Ladue", when I was momentarily distracted and virtually waylaid by a pint-size little white boy. Emerging from behind a rather large bush, the kid looked sternly up at me and in spite of my instant smile, said, "Hi, nigger. What's your name?"

Instantly, my young mind focused on the "nigger" insult and I snapped back, responding, "Hey–how you doin', you little peckerwood?"

Now, I didn't realize that, both, Frank and the kid's mother were close enough to hear the verbal exchange between me and the little boy or even if I would have reacted differently if I had known they were, but that thought was somewhat moot. They were both there and they both reacted differently, the mother especially.

Red-face and all, she came forward and verbally accosted me, yelling, "You didn't have to say that to him! He's just a five-year-old little boy and he doesn't know any better."

Frank stood by, looking stunned and somewhat subdued. However, I wasn't about to knuckle under and remain silent. I angrily addressed the woman, stating, "Well I'm just a twelve-year-old little boy and I don't know any better either. I just wonder who taught him the nigger word!"

The mother could hardly contain her anger. After blurting out, "Oh, you're one of those smart…," she then stifled her remark. My dander was surging even more at that point. I guestimated what she had squelched, asking, "A smart what–what?"

Of course, the lady refused to reply to me but I didn't really

Racism, Sexism, Trumpism, Pseudo-Christianity and the Cinema

care. I, then, turned to Frank, announcing, "I'm ready to go and I'll be waiting in the truck. I don't need her money!"

About forty-five minutes later, after I had simmered down and Frank had completed the grass cutting job alone, he joined me in the truck. I fully expected a tongue-lashing and I was poised to silently accept it. After all, since Frank was a native of Little Rock, Arkansas, I knew we held different opinions about race. However, his scolding was somewhat subtle and lackluster.

"You gotta git that chip off your shoulder," he began "White folks are born prejudiced, and they can't help it."

Since Frank was speaking in a matter-of-factly manner (he didn't even seem upset), I opted to reply to his statement. "Aw, Frank, that's not true. If that little kid's momma hadn't taught him the "nigger" word, he wouldn't know nothing about it. That woman is teaching her little boy to hate Negroes, and probably his old daddy too!"

"Maybe so," Frank sadly relented. "But it's how this old world is. Peckerwoods on top, and colored folks on the bottom–the very bottom."

"Well, it ain't right, Frank, I know that. And I don't understand it, I don't understand none of that stupid crap.

Reflecting back, I painfully shared that story with my elderly grandmother but I, alternately, regretted it. That's because she was weeping towards the end of it. I didn't exactly understand why but I didn't have the heart to press her on it. All I knew was that she was crying, and when I simultaneously thought back to the hurt expression on the face of the little kid that afternoon (he, too, was bawling when I headed for the truck), I emerged sorrowful also.

Admittedly, I am a sentimental man and I was a sentimental child as well. Therefore, in the aftermath of sharing the foregoing story with my grandmother, I longed to console her. Not uttering a word, I stepped forward and tightly embraced her that day.

And when she elected to hug me back, that is one of my fondest memories.

As a prelude to my next tale or account, I would like to cite something that's, both, inspiring and life-altering.

At least, that's my personal assessment.

Way back in 1963, when I was a young soldier stationed at Fort Sam Houston, Texas, I entered into an idyllic friendship that endures and thrives to this very day. That disclosure, in itself, is truly remarkable and priceless and I applaud the living God for graciously orchestrating it. Any twofold relationship that remains intact for a 55-year period is commendable (and that includes marriage), but when that subject alliance is comprised of a couple of individuals who are racially different, it is downright miraculous and celebratory too. And especially in a place called America.

When I first met "Tony" in the spring of 1963 (which happened to be the same year President John F. Kennedy was assassinated), I had already crashed head-on with military racism on three separate and painful occasions. That was somewhat noteworthy because, at that time, I had not even been in the army a full year. I had an invisible chip on my shoulder and I was very resentful of white folks in general. And being assigned to a work-place facility called the "Registrar," which was packed full with, both, military and civilian employees; most of them, Caucasian, did not set well with me. In fact, it depressed me.

However, owing almost exclusively to a young extraverted soldier named Anthony, I had a gradual change of heart, if not a magical metamorphosis. In less than a month's time, as Tony and I bonded during and after work, I prematurely came to embrace a concept that Rev. Dr. Martin Luther King Jr. most eloquently spoke about in the fall of that very year. It coerced me to regard my new found friend as a "visionary." Because, up until that point in my life (and, sadly, over a half a century later), Tony is the only white person who looked pass the color of my skin and embraced

Racism, Sexism, Trumpism, Pseudo-Christianity and the Cinema

the content of my character. And for that, I continue to cherish and love him with all my heart.

In July of 1977 I was 33 years old, single, self-sustaining (meaning, I was gainfully employed) and I had a nagging itch for travelling.

In past years, I had been to Los Angeles, California a couple of times, to Kansas City, Missouri, Chicago, Illinois, Indianapolis, Indiana and even Louisville, Kentucky, which was my friend Tony's birthplace. However, although I vacationed with Tony in his hometown in 1967, he no longer lived there in 1977, ten years later. Instead, he and his family (a wife and two kids) had moved back to San Antonio, Texas and my friend had become a police officer. Therefore, after I was discharged from the army in June of 1965, I didn't set foot back on Texas soil until the summer of 1977.

To our mutual joy and credit regarding that visit, neither of us had changed very much. Tony was the same congenial and talkative fellow I had grown to treasure over the years and I was the same demonstrative jokester I had always been. We talked for hours on top of hours, drinking our beer and laughing and reminiscing and never did a cross word emerge from our mouths. And oddly enough, that is acutely applicable to our ongoing friendship at present. Oh, we have disagreements from time to time (after all, Tony is now a retired cop and I've always been somewhat militant) but, still, we remain loving and civil to each other. And that is whether we're in San Antonio, in Saint Louis or conversing on the telephone, which is quite frequently.

Now, although the aforementioned is representative of our precious and storybook relationship, there are a stream of vivid memories that significantly mark our various visits over the years. And one of those reflections occurred in the midst of my summer visit in 1977.

When I first arrived in San Antone in July of that particular year, Tony was working the day–watch, and would be for a couple of more days. I was priorly aware of that factor and it was fine and dandy with me. After all, I had long known Tony's wife and we both loved to interact with each other. Fact was, I was in the picture when she and Tony were dating each other in San Antonio.

Therefore, when I hearken back to a certain morning that I've come to virtually savor, it transpired in an atmosphere that was serene and easy. To be specific, I was sitting on the couch in the living room, watching "The Price is Right" on television while Tony's wife was in the adjacent kitchen, preparing breakfast for the two of us. It was a cool, summer day, the air-conditioning unit was purposely cut off and the front door was propped opened. Actually, the door was off-side the living room, well within my view and the only thing that might dissuade an intruder from entering the house at-will was the screen door. However, it wasn't even latched.

As I mentioned above, I could clearly see the greater outdoors, looking through the screen door from my vantage point on the sofa. And, obviously, that view was quite reciprocal to random individuals who stood at the front door also. Because when a little white boy came into my view outside that door, standing affront a grown white woman, he excitedly declared what he was seeing.

"Momma–Momma, it's a chocolate man in there!" he shouted. "A real chocolate man, Momma!"

Even when the rather embarrassed mother took the liberty to pull open the screen door and proceeded to enter the house (it was apparent that she knew the home's residers), I was laughing almost uncontrollably. Furthermore, when I opted to rise from the couch and my on-site hostess (Tony's spouse) simultaneously emerged from the kitchen, I was momentarily groping for words.

Evidently, the woman was not. "I am so sorry, Sir," she firmly said. "Please forgive my little boy. He doesn't know that much about race. I sincerely apologize for him."

Finally, I stifled my laughter. "Miss, believe me," I replied, "I'm not offended in the least by what he said.

To be honest, I was once called the n-word by a little white boy around his age. It's kind of refreshing in a certain way. And as long as he doesn't come over and bites a chunk out of my arm, he is cool with me."

Of course, in the short aftermath of the foregoing episode, proper introductions were made and I came to enjoy the newly-arrived woman and her seemingly shy little boy. But before the kid left the house that day, thanks to my gentle prodding and kidding around, the youngster had come out of his shell. In fact, when we bided farewell to each other, he vigorously shook my hand–and didn't attempt to bite it. I sincerely hoped that his first one-on-one interaction with a black man would be a pleasant and long-enduring memory to him.

A RELEVANT REFLECTION

Admittedly, I am a huge movie buff and I always have been. It's not because I'm disenchanted with everyday life or because I struggle with boredom. On the contrary, it's because movies inspire me, encourages me to think and, ofttimes, pay homage to a myriad of principles I hold dearest. Referencing an assertion that's frequently voiced on television's TCM channel (Turner Classic Movies) it maintains that "Movies are an intricate part of who I am."

Therefore, when I take the time to reflect on American parents who callously endorses racial hatred to their innocent off springs (especially, the white ones), I find myself recalling a movie entitled "Rosewood." That's the film (based on a true story) when a Caucasian woman blatantly lies about a "colored" man sexually and physically assaulting her. And although the woman is secretly known to be a person of ill-repute, the white townspeople uses her fabrication as an excuse to viciously terrorize and slaughter the black people who live amongst them.

I especially remember the white father and son who were highlighted in that film.

As one of the leaders of that vengeful white mob, the dad not only scolded his boy for merely "playing" with a black youngster, he gleefully executed several "colored" victims right in front of him. Seemingly, the father deemed it a teachable moment.

But that was not the height of the father's degenerate behavior. In, yet, another scene the man actively prods his little boy to strike the backside of a stationary horse. Not for sport, but because the horse's owner, who was a black man, was sitting atop the steed with restrained hands and a noose around his neck.

Now, I don't know if the white community still plays host to vile creatures like the father depicted in "Rosewood," but when I focus on a young man named Dylan Roof (the infamous white boy who went on a killing spree inside an Afro-American church) and then progress on to recollect the Caucasian teenager who randomly slew 17 high school kids in Parkland, Florida in February of 2018, I can't help but wonder. Reportedly, that godless shooter, too (like Roof}, was a budding white supremacist. Neither of those boys were born with racist mind-sets. Some hate-filled adult (or adults) implanted that seed inside them and proceeded to fertilize it as well. And if the sower of that seed called him or herself a "parent" while doing so, he or she is seriously mentally-ill and grossly delusional.

Even before I became elderly myself, I staunchly believed that young people should respect and virtually revere older people, and especially when those older people happened to be their parents or guardians. But today is a new day! When a church pastor stops following Christ and embarks upon his own alternate path, then it's time to stop following him. Likewise, when a parent strays off the beaten path and no longer strides towards righteousness and justice, it's time to stop tagging along behind them also. And children must take note: One day they will be in that parental role and if they are not intent upon implanting the "best" part of themselves inside their offspring, then they are undeserving of that stellar title. An authentic parent should strive to enhance their child's being, not sabotage or hinder it.

Am I advocating open rebellion or disobedience when it comes to parents or guardians? No! I am simply saying that when your heart tells you that something or some one (anyone) is grossly wrong, you are obliged to champion that which is right. That was the collective cry of those grief-stricken kids in Parkland, Florida in February of 2018. They realized that something has desperately gone awry in America, that so-called adults are acting irresponsibly, and they decided to step up to the plate. They are adamant about changing current gun laws and banning assault rifles and decreasing weaponry ownership in our country. And I only pray that they're resilient and long-suffering in their cause.

A RELEVANT REFLECTION

When I was a child of 7, my dad instructed me to do something that I didn't have the stomach nor the heart to do. Grasping a live chicken in his hand, he ordered me to take it and proceed to our front lawn. There, he further told me to "wring" the chicken's neck. Naturally, that would render the fowl dead, my mother would then pluck its feathers and, alternately, prepare it for dinner.

Without much thought, I flatly refused. In fact, I replied, "No, Sir, that chicken hasn't done anything to me. I'm not mad at it."

Even my old man laughed before scolding me and putting a strap to my backside. The punishment aspect was my only regret that afternoon. Although my dad vowed he wasn't going to let me eat any of the fried chicken, my mother interceded and dad eventually recanted. I was glad because I always loved chicken and steaks. I was also glad I didn't have to go out and shoot a cow.

Three Strikes and You're out–One

Well before my dear friend, Tony, decided to relocate to San Antonio, Texas and eventually became a police officer, I seriously entertained the idea of becoming a lawman myself. It wasn't because I wanted to be a bad-ass, a fearless hero or even because I dreamed of being a champion for law-abiding citizens. To be perfectly candid, it was solely due to where I was working at that precise time. Specifically, I was a 23-year-old clerk who worked at the Central District Police Headquarters, located in downtown St. Louis, Missouri.

Looking back, I earnestly believe I would have become an exemplary police officer. I've always been conscientious and passionate in regards to every role I played in life and I'm certain I had something special to bring to the table in that venue also. However, in the wake of three back to back to back happenings; diverse circumstances that were practically steeped in racism and asinine biasness, my desire to become a cop gradually dissipated and left me reeling in a state of wonder and anguish.

Now, it is said that, "time heals all wounds" but that is farcical and just plainly untrue. Some wounds, especially mental ones are with you until the day you die. And they remain open and festering because of a very prominent, insidious feature. That feature is called "injustice" and all the time in the world cannot vanquish or erase it from your heart. If one of your dear loved ones perishes unjustly (due to school massacres, drive-by shootings, police executions, etc.) there is no lasting solace and no "getting over it" because down deep, when you're alone with your thoughts, you truly know that your murdered loved one was underservant of his or her terrible fate.

Therefore, when I painfully relive a trio of incidents that took place way back in 1968, when I contemplated joining the police force, the foregoing analysis still remains fixed in my mind.

I sincerely hope in the midst of my effort to transport the reader back to that sad and ominous year (notably, it earmarked the slayings of, both, Dr. Martin Luther King Jr. and Sen. Robert F. Kennedy), it will resonate in your hearts and minds also. That is the very essence of compassion and empathy and without those

Racism, Sexism, Trumpism, Pseudo-Christianity and the Cinema

two qualities we are a nation, wandering in the wilderness. Again, I encourage people to cast aside their blinders. And as you picture the forthcoming scenario (especially white individuals), try to imagine yourself in my shoes:

When I was but four years old, I suffered horrendous pain from a malady called "strep throat". And being the child I was at the time, I was crying profusely and uncontrollably. However, I wasn't alone in my severe physical agony. My father, while holding me ever so tightly, was weeping as if my pain was critically wracking his own body. That poignant scene (the transference of hurt and anguish between a loving dad and his ill son) would occasionally replay it self for only five additional years. Underlying reasons notwithstanding, when I turned nine years old my father gradually and almost-entirely vanished from my life. Despite his faults, I loved him dearly.

Now upon fast-forwarding another nine years, when I was a soldier in Uncle Sam's army, I am hopeful the reader of this account will, alternately, get the gist (or, the connect) of what I disclosed above, as well as what I am on the verge of divulging.

Shortly after completing high school in June of 1962, I elected to enlist in the military service. And when I did, I felt fortunate and blessed to form a rather rapid and close-knit alliance with a fellow black St. Louisan whom I came to fondly call "J". Subsequently, as J and I was subjected to the toil and rigor of basic training and looked forward to graduating from that forerunning initiative, an unforeseen and life-altering snag occurred. In less than two weeks prior to the graduation ceremony, I was stricken with a severe, agonizing disorder which was later diagnosed as a "bowel obstruction".

Well, upon cutting-to-the-chase, while I was literally writhing in excruciating stomach pain and, simultaneously, pleading with J not to summon an ambulance (even in my misery, I was bent on graduating on schedule), I eventually lost consciousness. All I vividly recall about that grueling episode was my lying supine on my barracks bunk, watching J as he frantically ran to-and-from the outlying latrine, seeing him gingerly applying hot towels to my extended abdomen and, most prominent of all, observing J as he was practically bawling his eyes out.

Then, in the short interim, I was hurriedly operated on, promptly hospitalized and was later informed that I was fortunate to be alive. During my two-week stay in the U.S. army Hospital, J didn't miss a single day visiting me. That, too, endeared me to my friend.

As it would play out, the emergency surgery I under went in basic training would prove to be somewhat detrimental to my cherished relationship with J. To our mutual regret, J was eventually sent overseas (Korea) while I remained state side (Fort Sam Houston). And although we corresponded faithfully with one another during our separation, there was a resurgence in our friendship when we both bade farewell to the U.S. Army in the mid 1960s.

As the succeeding years unfolded, my camaraderie with J remained intimately fixed and almost vital. In 1968, although J had married and had fathered a child, we both relished our civilian status and still interacted regularly.

Also, in '68, after working over a year as a "Prisoner Processing Clerk" at Saint Louis city's Central District, I took the police officer examination and easily passed it. Incidentally, I appeared before the verbal interview board, wearing a suit I had borrowed from J.

Essentially, after hurdling over the two hiring mechanisms (the written and verbal exams), I was slated to join the ranks of an upcoming police training cycle. Not so surprisingly though, before I could commence classes at the law enforcement academy, I was compelled to present a valid driver's license. However, since I didn't own a car, I didn't possess one and began to take steps to secure one. I, of course, viewed that prerequisite as a minor setback. However, that's when things began to go awry and when

Racism, Sexism, Trumpism, Pseudo-Christianity and the Cinema

my law enforcement aspirations began to gradually corrode. My culminating disenchantment was emotionally traumatic, exasperating and life-changing.

Now, whether it could be attributed to pure irony or mere coincidence, the onset of my disillusionment with the law enforcement apparatus had very much to do with a driver's license— and a 1968 stick-shift Ford Mustang. But it wasn't about my non-existing license, it was about my friend J's previously suspended driver's license. Unfortunately, J was driving on a traffic ticket (which he was protesting) and his wife, similar to me, was not a driver. And all of the aforementioned is relevant because as events would play out, "misfortune" would proceed to take a virtual nosedive and, then, rapidly spiral downward. It dramatically commenced in the midst of my visiting J and his family, which is something I did ever so often.

In spite of having a relatively new car, J and his wife (along with their newly-born son) resided in a cold-water flat, located near downtown St. Louis. Therefore, when J became feverish and gravely ill one evening, it was a wise and reasonable choice to seek medical aid at a hospital which was less than thirty minutes away. City Hospital No. 1, which was located on the city's south side, was practically a straight shot from my friend's house and with a minimal amount of turns.

Well, in hindsight, I wish I had summoned an ambulance. J's home was void of a telephone (something that was common for blacks in those days) but, still, I imagine I could have found a phone booth somewhere in the not-too-distant vicinity.

Then again, although J was continually grimacing in pain and perspiring heavily, he insisted that he could successfully execute the trip. Immediately, his wife and I were jointly skeptical and frantic! (As J was cringingly grasping his stomach area, I, of course, was vividly reliving my own yesteryear ordeal in basic training). But since time was of the very essence, we collectively shied away from counter argument and prepared for the trip to the hospital.

We hurriedly grabbed our jackets, J's spouse bundled up her five-month old baby (it was chilly outside) and, shortly, the four of us were aboard the Mustang, enroute to our intended destination.

But within a mere fifteen minute's time, our intentions were soundly dashed, both, dramatically and coldly. Practically slumping over the steering wheel (and maneuvering the car's stick), J inadvertently ran a red light and, almost instantaneously, a flashing light appeared directly behind us. J soon pulled over to the curb and I, who was sitting in the rear seat, was out of the vehicle in a minute's time. Admittedly, in my youngness and naivety, I, actually thought I had some clout or, at least, a leg up on an ordinary, average citizen. After all, my ongoing tenure with the police department was nearing two years. Unfortunately, my illusion was short lived. And it ended quite rudely when one of the two white officers addressed me. The lawmen, too, had climbed out of their squad car and were converging on the Mustang.

"Nigger, git your black ass back in the damn car!" the cop yelled. "You weren't told to get out!"

I was taken aback, insulted and mortified at the same time. I had difficulty digesting what the lawman had said. That is, until the younger cop spoke up, coming across just as crude and hostile as his partner.

"Didn't you hear what Officer Sims said?" he shouted. "Get yo' black ass back in the goddamn vehicle!"

I was clearly shaking my head in disbelief when I responded.

"Look fellas, my friend is seriously ill, he might even die!" I argued. "We're trying to get to the hospital! But why? Why are you talking like that? Hell! I work for the police department myself, just like you guys. I can show you my employment ID."

"We don't give a shit where you work, boy!" yelled the younger officer. "Git back into the car, fella, and now! Damn it!"

Although I was still shaking my head in disbelief, I sadly realized I was wasting my breath at that point. And besides that, the senior lawman was silently standing with his hand firmly on

Racism, Sexism, Trumpism, Pseudo-Christianity and the Cinema

his firearm. Subsequently, I returned to the Mustang as the cop duo flanked it from the rear. They, then, focused their attention on J.

Now, to be perfectly honest, I wasn't at all sure if my best friend could have resumed the road trip even if he had been given the opportunity to do so. Even as his distraught wife openly wept and resorted to profanity as well, J was saturated with perspiration and reeling in agony. However, my uncertainty proved to be moot. Alternately, J was placed under arrest, handcuffed and carted off to jail. The traffic citation he possessed was disregarded completely.

In reality, I later thanked God in light of where J was taken for incarceration. He was promptly taken to the Central District, which happened to be my staple work site. Within momentary delay, I could not refrain from repeatedly shaking my head (for the world of me, I cannot remotely comprehend human cruelty and blatant callousness!), I sought out headquarter's on-duty Watch Commander, a white officer I knew as "Capt. Parr." I rapidly pleaded my case to him, detailing everything that had happened up to that juncture, and I was able to arouse the captain's compassion and sense of fair play.

Parr arranged for J' instant release, alerting me that my "buddy" would still have to answer to the traffic charge, and soon J was transported to City Hospital No. 1. I, later, thanked the captain for his indulgence and timely intervention.

Well, as time marched on forward and J was treated, mercifully relieved of his gut-wrenching misery, I could finally vanquish my anxiety and depression. J had been diagnosed with a medical condition called a "fecal-impaction" and it was a disorder I had heard of. My mother, being a former hospital attendant, had eye-witnessed a teenaged boy succumb to it. And her rather emotional account had remained forever fixed in my very emotional mind.

Now, we all know that life is full of potholes, missteps and obstacles; that we sometimes, erect ourselves. "To err is human." And I certainly buy into the adage, "Into everyone's life–a little rain must fall." But I have always been in total awe of individuals who are, seemingly, unmoved and insensitive to the suffering of fellow human beings! Unless a person is sociopathic by nature, I cannot understand brazen dispassion in the face of life-and-death situations and regardless of racial biasness! And more relevant, that particular individual surely should not have a pistol on his hip and be attired in a police uniform.

That was my lingering outrage after that harrowing run-in with those two city cops; and I wasn't about to chalk it up as just another day. Therefore, I decided to write a scathing letter to the official powers that be denoting everything that took place on that subject evening; and the following is an explicit recap of what transpired afterwards:

Forthrightly, I was granted a secluded, man-to-man meeting with a "Colonel Bronston", who was the police chief at that particular time. The officer began to speak, but only after introducing himself, briskly shaking my hand and offering me a seat across from his desk.

"Before we get to the meat of the matter, young man", he started off. "Let me commend you on the excellence of your letter. I wish even a fourth of my officers could write as well as you."

"Thank you, Sir." I replied, noticing my submitted letter atop the colonel's desk.

"We have a very disturbing matter before us," the sedate-faced chief spoke again.

"Disturbing and very controversial too. But I guess it all comes down to credibility. You see, Mr. H, there is diverse and conflicting testimony regarding this matter."

"And what? May I ask, is the conflict, Colonel? What are the officers saying about it?"

"Frankly, while my officer's stories basically match, your account goes in an opposing direction," the chief responded. "For instance, both officers swore you never even informed them that your friend was ill. Plus, they said you failed to tell them about

Racism, Sexism, Trumpism, Pseudo-Christianity and the Cinema

your work connection with the department. They both indicated it was news to them that you work downstairs in prisoner processing. Maybe, in your personal frenzy that night, Mr. H, you thought you had shared that information with them."

In the wake of sheer absurdity, I grimaced in hopelessness. "They are lying their butts off, Colonel, both of them," I bluntly stated. "I know it and you know it. And what? What did they say about the racial slurs? Did they insist they were perfect gentlemen on that evening too?"

"No, they admitted that in the heat of their own anger that night, they acted crudely and unprofessionally, the colonel conceded. "But your friend's wife, they said she was calling them all kinds of insulting and derogatory names. But they are genuinely sorry about their unfortunate behavior. And I read them the riot act, chewed 'em out soundly, the both of them. There's no acceptable excuse for officers resorting to ugly racial slurs, and no matter how nasty the common man becomes. And I personally apologize for them."

"One person can't apologize for another person, Sir," I remarked. "It means absolutely nothing. Colonel, why would I bother to write that letter? I mean after the fact? What would I have to gain? What?"

The chief displayed a wry grin. "I'm afraid I can't explain your motives, young man," he stated. "Maybe you're being vindictive, hoping you can get my two officers into hot water. Get them even fired, maybe. Who knows? Maybe you can enlighten me."

At that juncture, I elected to pursue another point, one that was gnawing at my mind. "Colonel, you keep saying my officers, I asserted "I imagine you're aware that I'm slated to attend the police academy in the near future and afterwards I'll be considered one of your officers too. Does that mean anything to you, Sir?"

"Mr. H, I am actually looking forward to you joining our ranks in the coming months" was the Chief's smiling response. "As I stated earlier, I believe you'll become an outstanding law officer, a real plus. But we're talking about the future here, something that may or may not materialize.

But the pair of patrolmen who are maligned in your letter, Well–they are already in the fold. So–the bottom line is this: It's my officer's two-fold testimony against your–your singular testimony. There are two of them and, up to now, they have no blemishes or complaints on their records. Therefore, Mr. H, I am compelled to give credence to their submitted versions of this misfortunate incident. And I am sincerely sorry regarding it all. Frankly speaking, this is a distraction I can do without."

In retrospect, when I was first informed of my impending meeting with the Chief of Police, I promised myself that I would not become emotional, and especially while the session was actively being conducted. "Keep your emotions well in-check," I told myself.

However, since I had always been dogmatic when it came to justice and fair play, I knew I would be hard-pressed to maintain my resolve. And, unfortunately, I was unable to suppress my tears when I grew weary of that staged and fruitless meeting.

I was in the process of rising to my feet when I commented, "It's the same old, exasperating story, isn't it? No matter what black people do and no matter what we say, we always get the shaft; the crap end of the stick. The white status quo remains unchanged, intact and entrenched."

"This incident has very little to do with race, Mr. H," the colonel frowned. "Even if you were Caucasian yourself, I would still be compelled to rule the exact, same way."

"Everything in this country, Sir, has to do with race", I replied. "It was prevalent when I was a soldier in the army and it's more than evident in civilian life." I opted to swipe at my tears when I added, "Colonel, my best friend could have died as a result of your officer's callousness and racist behavior on the night we're talking about. It probably means absolutely zilch to you, but I love J very much. And I don't know; I truly cannot imagine what I would have done if he had not survived; if I would have lost him due to white racist bullshit! And that completely terrifies me, makes my blood run cold! Because, up until now, I have always felt I had a fix on what I'd do whenever certain situations cropped up. Well, at any event, I need to get the hell out of here and right this instant. But thanks, thanks for your time and indulgence. It's been revealing."

Upon retreating from the Chief's office, and feeling defeated and frustrated, I vaguely recall the Colonel calling out my name. But I didn't halt my advance. After all, what was left to say? And what good would it do? NONE!

A RELEVANT REVELATION

In the short aftermath of my rather emotional meeting with Colonel Bronston, something somewhat odd came about.

Prior to our session, I had no personal relationship with the Chief of Police and I recognized him only from observing still photos of him and, occasionally, viewing him on various local TV newscasts. And, yet, when I resumed my work role in the "Prisoner Processing" division (located downstairs in the Central Headquarters complex), I was frequently subjected to casual, "pop-in" visits from the police force's top officer.

Obviously, my uniformed co–workers (all of them, Caucasians) were impressed and honored in the wake of the Chief's impromptu appearances, but I was not. Even when he singled me out and essentially engaged in "small-talk" (ofttimes encouraging me to expedite my police academy plans), I was somewhat cheerless and standoffish as well. Eventually, after being subjected to two more demoralizing and disenchanting happenings, I informed him that my law enforcement aspirations were all but dead. Colonel Bronston appeared to be genuinely disappointed on that day. And as weird as it might sound, I actually felt sorry for him. But in another sense, I was truly heartened by his reaction. In all my years,

I had never interacted with a Caucasian man, especially one of prominence, who showed any semblance of remorse or humility. To say the least, it was refreshing!

Three Strikes and You're Out–Two

Although the foregoing account was insightful and quite mind-boggling to boot (at least, to me), it was not the lone factor that squelched my ambitions to become a lawman. To a certain degree, my run–In with those two biased officers emboldened me. I knew I was born with a moral leg-up on that pair. But a couple of months after that confrontation with those cops, my aspirations were besieged once again.

Just so happened, on April 3rd of '68, I observed my 24th birthday. I celebrated it with the usual fanfare (a cake, ice cream, lots of laughter and drinking beer with select friends) and I emerged somewhat subdued and inactive on the following day. After all, I was due to report to work at eight on the next morning, which was the 5th of April. However, as I sat in front of my television on the evening prior, relaxing and practically falling asleep, I was suddenly jolted awake by a breaking news flash.

Reverend Dr. Martin Luther King Jr. was murdered by an unknown assassin in Memphis, Tennessee.

Naturally, being an individual of strong sentiment, I was heartbroken and instantly reduced to tears, but I was not remotely surprised by the event. I loved and admired Dr. King and I was well aware of what he stood for. But as a soldier stationed in Texas in 1963, I lived through the killing of President John F. Kennedy, I grieved over the shooting of Medgar Evers in Mississippi and the slaying of Malcolm X in New York City, so nothing surprised me about the "evil that lurks in the hearts of man."

But what did surprise me and give me momentary pause (however, only slightly) was what transpired when I returned to my

Racism, Sexism, Trumpism, Pseudo-Christianity and the Cinema

work site on the morning of the 5th. To be perfectly candid, I really expected my white co-workers to treat the Dr. King assassination as a nonentity. Honestly, I rather hoped that would be the case. I've never cared for insincerity or false pretense. However, I didn't anticipate a mocking song and an atmosphere of subdued glee. When I came on the scene, my supervising sergeant had his back turned to me and he was joyously entertaining a couple of his fellow officers. Sporting a monotone voice, he hearkened back to a memorable tune from the "Wizard of Oz" movie. Apparently though, he couldn't recall the original lyrics. His improvised version was, "Ding-dong–the king is dead. Which old king? Martin Luther King. Ding-dong–the wicked king is dead…"

Well, at that juncture the sergeant was made aware of my sudden presence. Then, upon turning and facing me, he casually stated, "Aw, I didn't see you standing there. Ah didn't mean nothing by my little song. Jest foolin' around." My somber response was, "I do believe you didn't see me, sergeant." Then, without further ado or dialogue, I walked off and soon began my eight-hour workday.

In reality, I could have been highly upset or appalled by my supervisor's insensitive and celebrant behavior in the brief aftermath of Dr. King's assassination but, strangely enough, I wasn't. A very wise, elderly lady (my own mother, in fact) oftentimes told me that, "In the wake of idiotic remarks and actions, take a moment to consider the character of the main source." So, upon recalling several occasions when I was "invisible" (meaning, not in plain view), wherein I realized that the sergeant had no qualms in spewing out the so-called "N-word" or the term "jigaboo" as well, I was able to suppress my disgust.

In addition, at that particular time, another very relevant adage popped into my mind. And, by mere coincidence, it came from the mouth of a sergeant also. But the referenced spokesman, a Sgt. Andrews, was not a law officer, but a fellow noncom in the U.S. army. My soldier comrade was fond of saying, "It is better to remain silent and have others think you're a fool–than to open your mouth and remove all doubt." Therefore, as voices from my past rushed forward, gradually comforting me and yielding me a very simplistic perspective too, I was able to come to grips with my supervisor's coldness. As pathetic as it was, the police sergeant was just being himself.

Admittedly though, my heart was not remotely at peace. The evil that precipitated my supervisor's song was a vexation that fostered so many questions it would take hours to answer them. For example, although I never entertained the thought of asking the officer point-blank (I was bent upon keeping my distance from the man), I could not refrain from trying to assess his underlying Psyche! I truly wondered, if given the chance to expound on the topic, could the lawman, himself, explain his apparent hatred for Rev. Dr. King.

Then again, hatred is one thing but relishing the demise of a living being (someone you've never met) is another matter altogether. Could the sergeant credibly justify his overt jubilation regarding the civil rights leader's violent murder? And if he could do so, if he could justify his blood thirst on behalf of a person who had done no harm to him per se, then what measure of punishment would he crave for an individual who directly offended him?

Seriously, would the sergeant yearn to boil the man in oil? Would he desire to tar and feather his offender? Would he delight in seeing his antagonist being dragged behind a pick-up truck: Or, would he stick to an age-old tradition? Would he be fully sated in seeing his transgressor lynched and dangling from a tree? Of course, none of the foregoing measures would be particularly unique or too extreme to invoke. In the hearts of classic, well-seasoned racists, any one of those punitive mechanisms would be considered sufficient. And, tragically, many people of their vile persuasion would dare to identify themselves as "Christians." And

Racism, Sexism, Trumpism, Pseudo-Christianity and the Cinema

that, in itself, prompts a follow-up query. "Is there such an animal as a "Christian racist?"

Now, that question is open to real, in-depth debate but since it's addressed in my upcoming segment that I entitled "Pseudo-Christianity, I choose to temporarily put it on the back burner. In reality, I wasn't prolongly devastated by my supervisor's celebratory behavior regarding the King assassination in April of 1968.

Two months later, in June, the sergeant was just as pleased in the aftermath of the Robert F. Kennedy slaying. In borrowing a term from modern day vernacular, maybe the sergeant was just a perennial hater. I just made an everyday effort to keep my distance from him.

Three Strikes and You're Out Three

My clerical position in the "Prisoner Processing" division paired me with a select group of seasoned law officers; all of them, white, and all of them, adept in the craft of fingerprinting. After undergoing that procedure, "suspects" were then photographed (the so-called mug shot) and, subsequently, instructed to take a seat next to my adjacent desk. That was the traditional "booking process." Once there, as they sat affront me, I encouraged the man or woman to be totally honest (reminding them that fingerprints don't lie) and typed up a trio of cards on them. All of the cards were distributed amongst the various law enforcement agencies; one for the city (locally), one for the state and the other, federal.

Although it may sound rather pompous or braggadocious, I was exceptional when it came to my job. Not only was I always on time, I was well-organized, proficient and adept at interviewing suspects. However, I wasn't the only person who was impressed by my job performance. An officer I'll identify as "Elliot" felt likewise. In fact, as time went forward, Elliot and I bonded and we mutually agreed to synchronize our work shifts. That meant we became a one-two combination.

Now, if it is not obvious by now, I am a great believer in friendship. In my estimation it's as priceless as the "Hope Diamond." I also believe that good people are at a premium in this world. Although Elliot was white, I began to see benevolent qualities in him. And, apparently, the feelings were mutual. And Elliot didn't mind telling me so.

With all of the foregoing said, as I inch towards the fabled "straw that broke the camel's back," which was the third and final circumstance that shattered my desires to attend the police academy (in reality, it was left solely to my discretion), I am poised to divulge what specifically transpired. Oddly enough, I actually welcomed interacting with newly-arrested individuals and inmates alike and, as time went by, they seemingly warmed up to me also. For one thing, contrary to my fellow clerks and officers-in-charge too, I wasn't judgmental or uncaring regarding their expressed woes and claims of innocence. (Need I indicate that the majority of the prisoners were black and my co-workers were all white?) Considering sheer volume and factoring in the race component, I reasoned that a certain segment of the incoming suspects were not guilty of the charges they faced.

Regardless though, I was obliged to sympathize with a number of them (whites, also), simply because I wasn't a member of a selected jury. In reflection, it would have been nice to have worked amongst uniformed individuals who felt similarly. Seemingly though, my co-workers felt that all recently-arrested men and women (again, whites also) were "guilty until proven innocent."

I would derive pleasure from reporting that my close-knit cohort, Elliot, was not included in the forestated group, but I cannot. He seemed to be in lockstep with them. I figured, similar to some of his fellow officers, he was suffering from burn-out. Moreover, he seemed to share their mind-set when it came to the prostitution community too and, eventually, it was that factor that

Racism, Sexism, Trumpism, Pseudo-Christianity and the Cinema

pitted us up against each other. That fateful incident took place in the wee hours of a Sunday morning and right in the middle of a weekly, routine tradition. Every late Saturday and early Sunday mornings prostitutes were randomly rounded up and arrested by roving police personnel. And, of course, they were brought to the Prisoner Processing division, located in downtown Saint Louis.

In reality, it was no big deal because Elliot and I were well aware of that traditional, weekend operation. We had coped with it quite a few times in the past. Elliot fingerprinted, took the mugshot and I typed, nothing out of the ordinary.

I usually engaged in brief conversations with various arrestees but since there was such a large influx of so-called "ladies of the night" on those particular mornings, I restricted my verbal remarks to a single but very important question. Very emphatically, I would ask each suspect, "Have you been arrested before?"And if, perchance, they replied "No," I would pose the query once again.

On the morning I'm recapping, I was finally taking a breather at my desk and Elliot walked over to me, holding a record folder. He was highly pissed off.

"Didn't I hear you tell this bitch that fingerprints don't lie?" he asked me. "And she claimed she hadn't been arrested? I hate a lying ass whore! She got a record a mile long!"

I grasped the folder, saying, "I asked her two times."

Man, I had a feeling she was lying through her damn teeth, a sorry-ass heifer. Asked her two times."

"Well, her ass is gonna be even more sorry when I git her back out," Elliot vowed. "And it won't have no reflection on you."

Upon leaving the file with me, Elliot soon returned to the fingerprinting section. I thought—"Why on earth would a professional prostitute deliberately lie about her arrest record, fully aware that she'd probably be released within the next four hours?" That was, both, common and traditional and, alternately, explained why it was quite possible to process the same female suspect twice within an eight-hour work period. Then, a second query arose in my mind. Prior to walking away, my officer friend opted to also say, "It won't have no reflection on you." Totally confused and perplexed, I had no inkling of what he meant. I recall thinking, "It makes no sense, none whatsoever!"

As it would come to pass though, it made perfect sense–to Elliot. It all came rather dramatically together when the fibbing prostitute herself returned to our section to be reprocessed.

Appearance–wise, the 25-year-old woman was somewhat homely, disheveled, aschen-looking, dark-complexed and, of course, Afro-American. In addition, she was solemn and obviously afraid and I, despite my inner anger, could not help pitying her.

Evidently though, my work-partner, Elliot, was entirely void of any feelings that resembled mine. Instead, he was infuriated and intent upon giving the suspect the harshest scolding of her young life. It was then that I came to realize why he had previously announced, "It won't have no reflection on you."

Elliot initiated his verbal tirade as he forcefully snatched the prostitute's wig off her head. He ignored the woman's outcry completely when he yelled, "Look at your stinking ass, ain't washed your goddamn hair in months! You ugly, funky, black-ass NIGGER bitch! Who the hell would pay out good money to screw you? Git your disgusting ass over here!"

To be honest, the foregoing dialogue was just an excerpt from Elliot's vociferous rant. There was more to it. However, I cannot recall the text verbatim because my mind was essentially frozen on the "nigger" term. I wasn't cognizant of what else Elliot said and, at that point, I didn't really care about it. Inwardly, I just felt sad; sad for myself, sad for the subject prostitute (she was actively weeping) and, strangely enough, sad for my angry co–worker too.

There's no way to get around it. I've always been a creature of deep emotions (and I'm pretty sure that's evident by now) and I make no excuses or apologies for it. Therefore, when Elliot finished up his reprocessing chores and, then, sent the wailing woman over to my desk, I, too, was tearful.

Racism, Sexism, Trumpism, Pseudo-Christianity and the Cinema

I turned to my typewriter as the suspect sat down before me, and my concerned co-worker approached my position as well.

"What's the matter with you?" he asked me. 'What gives? I mean—why are you upset?" In the throes of my despair, I was momentarily shaking my head. "Can we talk a little later, Elliot?" I responded. "You know when we're by ourselves?"

Exhibiting a certain degree of reluctance, Elliot went on to honor my request to talk "a little later." Then, a couple of hours later, when the suspect flow petered out altogether, that proposed discussion got underway. I had regained my composure considerably but I was still disheartened. Sitting in the chair reserved for incoming arrestees, Elliot opened up the conversation.

"Okay, let me have it straight," he said. "What did I do that struck you so wrong—it made you feel sad? What was it?" I took a deep breath, but it was hardly due to exhaustion. "Let me ask you something, Elliot" I began. "If a white prostitute came through here, and she lied—just like that Franklin woman did (I had remembered the suspect's name), would you have yanked her wig off too? Dogged her out too?"

"A whore is a whore," Elliot frowningly remarked.

"I don't give a care if they're green or blue—or polka dot. Is that what this is all about, race? Skin color don't matter to me, and you should know that. Aw, buddy-boy, I care about you!"

I could not cast off my solemnness. "Is that why you bothered to forewarn me?" I questioned "And why you said it won't have no reflection on me?" Elliot paused a moment to ponder, allowing me to add, "You just had to say it, didn't you? You couldn't help saying the "nigger" word. Seems like it's always on the tip of white folk's tongues. I don't get it, and I never have got it."

Elliot appeared to be flustered. "But it's just a word, kiddo," he offered. "And it doesn't have any bearing on our relationship. I would never call you that."

"Even if I happen to piss you off someday, Elliot?" I asked. "What then?"

"Not ever, guy. I value our friendship much too much. And if it means anything to you, I am sorry. I apologize. I didn't mean to hurt you, or offend you.

So, can we git over this and still be friends?"

When my cohort offered up his apology, he also extended his hand to me. I reluctantly joined in the hand clasp, but my mind was momentarily elsewhere. I recalled that one-on-one meeting I had once had with Colonel Bronston, the Chief of Police. The colonel, too, suggested that we bury the racist-inspired issue and, then, ride off into the proverbial sunset. Unfortunately, though, in regards to many Afro-Americans, a similar vexation is, ofttimes, on the horizon.

Seemingly, Caucasians emerge oblivious (or unconcerned) of most racially-connected problems and stand ready to dismiss them entirely. Plainly speaking, if it doesn't impact their privileged lives, it's unimportant to them. Over the years I've come to believe that many of them are void of empathy.

Down deep, that was my personal assessment regarding Elliot's actions during the prostitute episode. I asked him if he would have behaved the same way–if the woman had been white instead of black. He promptly denounced the racial factor and I gave him the benefit of the doubt. However, there was a particular aspect of that happening that weighed heavily on my mind.

In actuality, I could appreciate Elliot's seething irrateness (no one enjoys doing double work), I was even able to come to grips with his decision to rip off the woman's wig and berate her with profanity, but I could not reconcile with the "premeditation" measure. When Elliot took the initiative to forewarn me that his upcoming words would have "no reflection" on me, he was intent upon mouthing the "nigger" insult and I couldn't bring myself to reckon with it. Less than a month after that incident, I secured

Racism, Sexism, Trumpism, Pseudo-Christianity and the Cinema

a position with the Saint Louis Public Schools and never looked back—until now.

A RELEVANT REFLECTION

When I was a soldier stationed at Fort Sam Houston, Texas, I celebrated my 20th birthday (that was in the year 1964) and when I did I received a number of congratulatory tokens and verbal salutes. But not only from my mobile army barracks mates (I was assigned to the 24th Evacuation Field Hospital) but from a select group of co—workers at the Registrar's office on post. I even received a card, twenty bucks and a batch of doe-baked cookies from my mom a couple of days prior.

However, when I reflect back on that particular day, I zone in on one, stellar happening. And although many people will brand it trivial and unremarkable too, it is a happening that I dearly cherish to this very day. I had received a commemorative birthday card from my Afro-American homeboy, J, earlier in the week (he was then stationed in New Mexico) and it especially warmed my heart.

For I dearly loved J and prized his friendship. But the same heartfelt feeling was applicable to the only Caucasian individual I had come to call a "friend" also. Tony didn't allow my special day to go by unheralded either. In fact, after treating me to lunch on that specific afternoon, he, too, presented me with a birthday card. Here in the year 2018 I still possess that card because it stated something that practically defines me. It simply reads:

"I know a certain person—who is as nice as he can be. He is always nice to everyone, but is especially nice to me."

Then, at the bottom of the card, it reads, "I love you, Barry" (which is my middle name) "Your friend always and a day—Tony."

As I mentioned earlier, the above disclosure may not be earth-shaking or a big deal to the average person, but to me, it says something very meaningful and profound. I truly believed my friend honestly felt that special way about me (and I still savor those words) but, frankly, I have always yearned for everyone to feel likewise about me and, to be even more frank, that desire extends to white people also.

However, when I am compelled to concede that skin color is overwhelmingly responsible for the national disconnect between black and white Americans, it, both, baffles me and depresses me.

When I step back and seriously dwell on how I wish others should regard me as a human being, I cannot avoid from retreating to a life-long helpmate of mine. Oddly enough, that helpmate is called the "cinema." And focusing on the topic at hand, the select movie that comes to mind is entitled "Man Without a Face." That film, starring Mel Gibson, is about a former schoolteacher (Gibson) who was seriously injured in an automobile traffic accident. As a result of that fiery car crash, which additionally claimed the life of a young student, Gibson emerged with a grotesquely scarred face. Notably though, scar tissue comprised only half of the teacher's face. The other half, however, showcased, well, Gibson's handsome face.

Plot-wise, it was bad enough that the teacher was saddled with his hideous facial distortion but, to compound his physical problems, he was eventually scorned and ostracized by his fellow townspeople. Not because of something he actually did, but because he dared to serve as a tutor to a young towns boy. Due to ugly innuendo, unfounded accusations and his facial distortion as well, he is judged harshly, but unfairly by the peoples around him. And as the story advances, Gibson is made to officially answer to his irate and gutter-minded accusers.

His verbal defense was poignant and quite memorable (at least, to me). Amidst a public forum and speaking to that pompous, judgmental group, the teacher tells them (and I'm paraphrasing here) that "You people are so fixated and focused on my badly scarred face, you really don't see me."

And although the movie was not about a black man or even

Racism, Sexism, Trumpism, Pseudo-Christianity and the Cinema

racism itself, Gibson's declaration was quite insightful and thought-provoking. When I first watched that film, it occurred to me that there really are people (mostly, white ones) who "Can't see the forest for the trees."

When I recall the pertinent words on that yesteryear birthday card presented to me by my close comrade, Tony, there is, yet, another film that vividly seeps into my memory bank also. But the message it conveys is not singularly about looking beyond a physical blemish or a person's skin color.

It clearly focuses, instead, on a quality called empathy and is a boisterous cry for justice and a sense of common decency.

The name of that movie is "A Time to Kill" and it starred Matthew McConaughey as an attorney named Jake Brigance. In it, the attorney audaciously defends a black man (portrayed by Samuel Jackson) for gunning down two white men in rural Mississippi. Since those two men viciously assaulted and brutalized the "colored" man's young daughter, the subsequent murders were an act of aggressive vengeance. Of course, it was an uphill battle for Brigance because, first off, the movie took place in the deep south and even more significant, he was pitted against a bigoted, all white jury. Similar to a popular adage, "Drastic circumstances call for drastic actions."

Therefore, instead of appealing to the jury's sense of decency, Brigance resorted to something that was totally unorthodox. He enticed the jury members to collectively close their eyes (they obliged him) and he softly provided them a blow-by-blow account of what the little black girl (the victim) had endured: The physical and mental anguish, the humiliation, everything. Then, upon cautioning the jury to keep their eyes shut, Brigance said, "And now pretend that the young black girl was a little white girl.

Personally, that struck a deep chord inside of me but, as I confessed earlier, I am a compassionate and sentimental man. Recalling that film's powerful and poignant ending, I always

Lionel Barry Harris

wondered if it remotely touched the hearts of the Movie-Viewing white populace. I truly hoped so.

By The Way… Down deep, I could not condone the murderous actions of Samuel Jackson's character in the movie "A Time to Kill.

I can understand his fury and anger but I could never endorse that degree of naked revenge. However, I do subscribe to the age-old belief that we, as human beings, reap what we sow.

And I staunchly believe, too, that blatant evil and injustice are subject to some kind of future comeuppance. And I'm not alluding to some mysterious and obscure punishment sphere called "Hell" or "purgatory" either. I sincerely believe that mankind is susceptible to a degree of payback or retribution while still residing on earth. Furthermore, I have stood witness to some of those rebukes and I don't mind sharing a particular one with you, this book's readers.

In October of 1968, after being thoroughly disenchanted with the urban police department of greater St. Louis, I started working for the inner-city's Board of Education.

I mildly regretted not becoming a cop but, after a while, I took it all in stride. And more significant, when I embraced my administrative position with the Saint Louis public schools (I worked in a high school setting for 34 years), I was certain I had found my niche. Being in the presence of so many young people; kids of different races, religions and mind-set, added renewed zeal and real purpose to my life. I felt very fortunate and blessed.

However, within seven months of my transference from the police department to my job with the city's Board of Education, a truly unexpected incident occurred that not only gave me momentary pause, it left me in a state of deep rumination and wonder.

In June of 1969 (as stated, I resigned from the P.D. in October of the previous year), I was dating a young lady who had secretly captured my heart. I wasn't sure how she actually felt about me but, like that little old ant, "I had high hopes." But at the time I'm recalling here, we were actively dating. And on one of those

Racism, Sexism, Trumpism, Pseudo-Christianity and the Cinema

particular dates, thanks to the indulgence of my close-knit pal, J, we ate a late evening meal at a restaurant located in downtown Saint Louis.

I said "thanks to the indulgence of J" because, in reality, we were in the second stage of a double date (We had seen a movie earlier) and J was the owner and driver of the vehicle we were riding in. Naturally, J's wife was the fourth party in our dating group and she occupied the passenger seat across from her husband. Meanwhile, my date and I sat in the car's backseat. Incidentally, the vehicle J was driving on that evening was the same '68 Mustang he possessed the previous year.

Upon ending our dining session that night, the four of us made our departure from the restaurant and headed for the car. Our stroll was quite brief, however, because the car happened to be less than thirty yards from the dining facility's main entrance. I took the initiative to open the door on the passenger's side, my young lady quickly climbed inside and scooted over to her far left side and, I, in turn, boarded the car myself. Soon, I sunk into my seat but I was completely unaware that J had not assessed the immediate scene in the way I had. To be precise, the tail-end of the car in front of J's automobile was situated approximately two yards away but, contrarily, the space directly behind J's auto was not at all yielding. In fact, there was a parked police motorcycle occupying it.

To my later regret, J's wife had settled into her seat and had taken the time to lock her door before it became clear to me that J had not remotely scanned the immediate area in the manner I had. And that oversight was even more evident when my friend shifted his stick to the reverse position and then hit the gas pedal.

Then, as we heard a loud crash, J was instantly alarmed. "What the hell was that?" he asked. "Man, I–I thought you saw that motorcycle back there!" I responded, almost apologetically. "A motorcycle?" my friend replied, keeping his car stationary. "Yeah, a darn police motorcycle,"I stated. "I'm sorry, J, I really thought you noticed it too."

I can't recall what I said after I issued my words of regret to my friend because my attention suddenly shifted elsewhere. I momentarily rolled the rear window down as a uniformed law officer emerged, frantically racing towards the car. And I realized instantly that it was none other than a former nemesis of mine and J's. To be specific, it was the senior lawman (the one named "Sims") who controlled the episode when a gravely ill J was pulled over and, subsequently, was arrested and jailed in the winter of 1968, the prior year.

Evidently, the patrolman immediately recognized me also because a split-second later, as our eyes met, we simultaneously exclaimed, "Aw shit!" (It was as if we had rehearsed it).

To say the very least, we were mutually flabbergasted and seemed to be grasping for follow-up dialogue. In my amazement and utter disgust, I was momentarily speechless.

But, soon, the onlooking motorcycle cop did find his voice.

Displaying a face of anger, the officer was in the throes of speaking when J guided his car forward and then opted to disembark it. Everyone present (me, J, the cop and the two women) had clearly heard the sound of crushed metal when J had pulled the car forward. It was an excruciating sound!

"Do us all a big favor!" the officer yelled, singling out J. "Git back in your damn car and just drive the hell away! Please, just go."

Although J's wife was angrily weighing in on the happening (something that irritated, both, me and my date), J said absolutely nothing. Instead, he promptly reentered his vehicle and soon left the scene of the accident. As he drove off, I looked out the back window and glimpsed the mangled remains of the motorcycle.

In the short aftermath of that stressful motor vehicle episode, I could not avoid reliving it over and over again. And when I recalled, too, the expression of disappointment on Col. Bronston's face when

Racism, Sexism, Trumpism, Pseudo-Christianity and the Cinema

I sternly informed him that I no longer wanted to become a police officer, I yielded to deep speculation.

It was more than obvious that Officer Sims was hell-bent on having nothing further to do with us, neither J and nor me. Why else, I asked myself, would he insist that we vacate the accident scene, unmolested and totally unscathed? In addition, how would he, alternately, explain such a bizarre occurrence to his superiors? And, of course, the Chief of Police was the head of that pertinent body.

That led me to speculate a degree further. Maybe, I thought (although there was no way for me to confirm it) the colonel did lend a certain credence to my year-old written complaint. In essence, despite my not being in the loop of knowledge, it was likely (or, at least, possible) that the motorcycle assignment was a form of punishment. Regardless though, at the end of the day, it was mere speculation on my part. Still, here in 2018 (50 years later), I sometimes wonder about it all. And even if I was slightly correct in my personal supposition, I applaud Col. Bronston. Although his final ruling went against me, I graciously esteem him for his integrity and sense of decency during that yesteryear matter.

"Spare Me From The Dumb Stuff"

When I take the time to seriously assess "racialism" and any other prejudgment entity, my mind spills over with one negative term after another. I vehemently denounce it as hateful, unsavory, ignorant, ungodly, stupid, despicable, illogical and a multitude of other derogatory put downs. In addition, I have no qualms in identifying and avoiding individuals who embrace and endorse racist ideology. In my opinion, they are shameful and demon-inspired human beings.

However, even though I have struggled with racial bigotry all my days, there is one component of it that, on occasion, sticks to my craw and almost compels me to shake my head in pure awe. While I'm positive that I'll never come close to comprehending racism itself, it practically drives me up a wall when naked and conspicuous dumbness is thrown into the equation also. And when the dumb aspect presents itself, it renders racialism even more despicable and ugly–if that is at all possible.

To get to the gist of what I'm talking about, allow me to cite just a few of my personal adverse memories. They might ring insignificant and trivial to the reader, even somewhat unbelievable, but to me, the person who lived amidst the pinpointed happenings, they remain vivid and exceedingly noteworthy. I wish I could, somehow, forget them.

Before I digress back to the year 1964 (again), when I was a soldier stationed at Fort Sam Houston, Texas, it is imperative that I acknowledge a certain fact. Owing to my mother's insightful and wise counsel, I've lived my life with an unwavering creed. My mom solidly believed in the phrase, "The good you do–will come back to you, and it doesn't cost very much," and I came to fully endorse her concept. She also cited, "Do right and right will come back to you," and I joyously bought into that belief also. But my mom's wisdom did not stop there.

The forestated principles are in line with Christian doctrine. However, my mother was a realist too. She knew it was foolhardy to keep your eyes fixed on the heavens while completely ignoring the many ills that plague earth. Therefore, being all too familiar with the age-old disease called racism, my mother did not pull punches while weighing in on that very prevalent topic either. And one of the memorable things she oftentimes told me (and I'm summarizing here) was, "Don't even expect fairness from white folks. The majority of them see us as inferior and stupid. They're taught that. So, if you have to rub elbows with them; school, work, whatever, you should always try and best them, rise above them. You still might fail, but at least try your hardest."

I took my mom's advice as gospel, especially when I elected

Racism, Sexism, Trumpism, Pseudo-Christianity and the Cinema

to enlist in the United States army after graduating from high school in June of 1962. And although the monthly pay was a mere $78.00 a month at that time (I even took the initiative to sign up for a $40.00 allotment), I still put my best foot forward. In translation, that meant that I was adamant in out-soldiering my white counterparts and my fellow minorities as well. And although I, sometimes, fell short in the physical prowess department, I excelled mentally and scholastically.

I was skilled in writing, I was blessed with an exceptional memory and I was a virtual quick-study. And in that aspect, I was cocky enough to believe that I was capable of matching every written exam I was subjected to. In addition, I prided myself in being ultra-proficient. At Fort Sam, whether I was in the field or at my work-place on post, I was skilled and expert in my job.

In one respect, I wished my mother's yesteryear advice had not emerged so accurate. (It shook the foundation of my faith). My mom had warned me that in spite of my efforts to outdo Caucasian people, certain failure still lurked in the shadows. And although I yielded to rationalization in light of several race-biased episodes that transpired in late 1962 and early 1963, I could not come to grips with it in 1964.

Once again, I shook my head in sheer rage. In March of '64, I, along with 9 other PFC's (Private First Class) competed for an E-4 stripe (either corporal or specialist-4) and when we did, we were all aware that a physical stripe or patch was not awaiting the named victor. More than that, we collectively realized, too, that in accordance to our individual performances during the testing process, a numerical list would be compiled. Plainly stated, the contestants would be placed on that respective list and would garner stripes as they came down the military pipeline,

I had already been awarded two letters of commendation in January of 1964, I was praised for running the Registrar office during field maneuvers and I traditionally tested well, therefore, when I was awarded the number one spot in the aftermath of the examination process, I was pleased but I wasn't surprised. But I couldn't resist smiling whenever I observed the promotion list in the display case outside the Headquarters compound. There it was, my name in the number one spot.

In less than two week's, an E-4 stripe did come down the military pipe and it was promptly awarded to–the Caucasian soldier who was ranked number two! To state that I was livid, is a gross understatement. I couldn't believe it! I was firstly informed about it by one of my barracks mates, but I didn't initially believe him. It was too bizarre, too frustrating and too damn unjust!

But, nevertheless, it was indeed true. Without rhyme or reason, with no warning whatsoever, my corporal stripe was boldly awarded to the number 2 ranked white soldier. I acutely saw the relevance too; it was sickeningly appropriate. Since I felt defecated on anyhow, it was fitting and proper that the stripe went to the "number two" testee.

As it turned out, I actively and aggressively protested. I raised a ton of sand, went up through the official chain of command and, alternately, I was besieged with so-called apologies and every flimsy and makeshift excuse a person could imagine. But at no level did any of the white men I met with (all of them, officers) admit to the racism and biasness that was so starkly evident. To me, it was an exercise in futility and although I did obtain my stripe a month later, I still remain vexed by it. Moreover, whenever I relive that long-ago episode, I cannot refrain from asking a common sense question. Such as–when that promotion board came together to compile that official list (and they surely knew I was black), why didn't they simply assign the number 2 white boy the number 1 position then?

After all, I wouldn't have been any the wiser. In addition, didn't those board members know they were racially biased from the git-go? That is why I deemed the entire affair dumb. It was without any merit, whatsoever.

Racism, Sexism, Trumpism, Pseudo-Christianity and the Cinema

As I continued my life's journey, I must acknowledge that the army did not corner the market on gross stupidity and marked dumbness. When the year 1983 rolled around, I had worked for the St. Louis Public Schools for approximately 15 years and I had 4 years of marriage under my belt. As I stated, I dealt exclusively with students at the high school level and I thoroughly enjoyed my administrative role. My official title was "book clerk-treasurer"(which was more or less a business manager) and I was paid a decent salary.

However, although my heart wasn't really in it, I became aware that the Board's Food Services division was in search of an office manager and I opted to apply for that position.

At that particular time, my immediate family consisted of me, my wife, a teen-aged son and a 2-year-old son and, therefore, since the pending position hosted an attractive starting salary, I felt it would shore up our living status. Plus, since we resided in a townhouse, we were in the market for a home of our very own.

I had an impressive work resume. I was a top student when I attended two different military schools, I left the service with the rank of sergeant E-5, I worked for the federal government, I managed a large janitorial company in the state of Indiana, I worked for the St. Louis Police Department, as well as the Potter Electric and Wagner Electric companies and while working 15 years for the Board of Education, I had harnessed 15 "excellent" evaluations; one for each of those years. In addition, I attended the community college a couple of years and worked part-time in the G.E.D. program.

Obviously though, the resume component was of little value to the group charged with hiring an office manager for Food Services. Oddly enough, it was hardly even mentioned. But what was touted as being key to the selection process was the slated written examination. However, when it was disclosed that I had scored 91 on it and my staunches competitor had made 75 (so, they said), it, too, plunged downward in importance.

Lionel Barry Harris

From the word say-go, I was well aware of what I was up against. The competitor I alluded to above was not only a competitor, he was a "preferred" competitor. Even worse, the individual who preferred him was none other than the long-time head of the Food Services Division. Reliable sources had informed me that my challenger was a white man of Greek heritage (I'll call him Mr. P) and he was a close-knit pal of the division's director. Therefore, the ongoing hiring mechanism was a farcical smoke-screen. In addition, one of my informant sources told me I was just a "pain-in-the-ass" obstacle.

I've said it before and I'll say it again—when I elected to apply for the office manager position—my heart was not in it. For I thoroughly enjoyed working with and around young people. But when I was apprised that I was just "spinning my wheels," I took on a self-assigned mission. It was more than likely I'd lose the impending fight, but I was bent upon getting in a few good left hooks.

As it turned out, the deciding factor in selecting the victor for the Food Services position eventually rested on a staged oral examination. I branded it "staged" because the judging panel consisted of the rather pompous Food Services director, his staple white secretary and a lone black woman. In my estimation, I could have spoken with the passion and eloquence of the Rev. Dr. Martin Luther King Jr. and I wouldn't have emerged the winner. Seemingly though, I had a fan in the Afro-American woman but she was the only one.

After voicing my boisterous protest, another panel was hurriedly assembled. It was three token men (two of them, black) and they were all puppets for the head-honcho of Food Services. After appearing before that hand-picked group, I walked away and proceeded to file a grievance with the Equal Employment Opportunity Commission (E.E.O.C) the next day.

Subsequently, as a number of consecutive weeks passed by, I guess one might say, "I had my day in court." In my presence, a team of commission attorneys "cordially" locked horns with

Racism, Sexism, Trumpism, Pseudo-Christianity and the Cinema

a group of lawyers representing the Board of Education and, eventually, they came to a consensus.

I was told by the opposing side that my complaints were not without merit. They also issued a makeshift apology to me. Then, one of the Board representatives made a remark that I deemed absurd and somewhat asinine as well. Wearing a sedate expression, he said, "It's unfortunate but Mr. P has been serving as the office manager for several months now. And It wouldn't be fair to try and remove him from that position at this time."

Of course, I jumped on that rationale with both feet.

"Fair?" I angrily responded. "Now, all of a sudden we're gonna start talking about being fair? Man, give me a break!"

At that point, one of the commission lawyers spoke up. "But there is a silver lining," he inserted, looking at me." They are willing to assure you that you "will get the next managerial position that opens up."

"You can count on it," offered, yet, another Board attorney. I sat, shaking my head in exasperation. "But don't you guys see?" I asked. "That's the damn problem. Why put people through a ton of bull crap changes—When there's always somebody waiting in the wings for the job? Who needs that kind of anguish in their lives? It's all so stupid and shady like. No, I don't want to be the dude waiting in the damn wings. So, it may sound a little crude, and so be it, but you guys can take that offer of your's and stick it where the sun don't shine. I don't appreciate it and I don't want it. No, thank you."

And that was essentially that. I was offered the supervisory job at the Board's warehouse a month later but I flatly turned it down. I was adamant about what I said to those attorneys during our final meeting and I never regretted it. Neither did I ever apply for another position.

By The Way —

When I filed that discrimination complaint with the EEOC, I was working in a high school that was headed by a principal who was obviously white. I inserted the term "obviously" because only a white person could come up with the rather dumb, lame-brain argument he expressed to me while the case was still ongoing.

Sporting a wide grin, he remarked, "I don't know how you can legitimately claim race-discrimination in your case because, after all, Mr. P is a Greek, a minority himself." I've always feared that my head would fall off one day, conversing with so many ridiculous Caucasians. I was shaking it to-and-fro when I replied, "When I was down south, I don't remember seeing any water fountain signs reading 'Greeks only.' I didn't see any restaurants or theaters indicating No Greeks allowed. 'I don't remember a damn governor blocking Greeks from entering a schoolhouse–and I certainly don't recall Greeks being hanged from trees, randomly murdered or tarred and feathered! So, man, what the hell are you talking about?"

"Well, I'm just saying…

"Naw, you're not saying anything," I angrily stated. "When you suggest that Greeks suffer racism just like Negroes do, you ain't saying shit!"

At that juncture, the principal was red-faced. He didn't like my tone or my bold manner. But I didn't much care. He should have kept his stupid reasoning to his self.

To be honest, when my immediate boss (the principal) took the liberty to vocalize his personal slant on my dealings with the EEOC, I didn't dismiss him as a classic racist.

I actually believed he was naive and he didn't know any better. Neither did I brand him remotely cruel or mean-spirited.

Certainly, I had been exposed to white individuals of the latter ilk and my boss seemed heads and shoulders above them. In fact,

Racism, Sexism, Trumpism, Pseudo-Christianity and the Cinema

after interacting with the man for nearly five years, I considered him to be a friendly and decent guy. He was far from perfect and he wasn't void of racial biasness either, but he was adept at keeping it in check.

But, unfortunately, I had dealings with Caucasian people who made my principal associate look like a saint.

And some of them, in their overt bigotry, did not even know me and had never laid eyes on me before. That analogy was so idly evident when, in the late nineties, my wife and I were returning from a road trip to the state of Nebraska.

We had enjoyed a five-day stay at the home of my wife's brother and his family in Omaha. (It was a trip we made every year). And while driving back to St. Louis, we elected to stop somewhere to eat lunch. At the pinpointed time, we were in the vicinity of St. Joseph, Missouri. I happened to have had a taste for fried catfish that particular afternoon and since I had glimpsed a billboard showcasing one of my favorite chain restaurants, I coaxed my wife into indulging me. Plus, I was the one at the steering wheel at that juncture.

Now I didn't think anything of it at the time, but if I had, maybe I would have made an alternative decision Then, again, maybe not. But I did experience a funny feeling when I finally drove onto the restaurant's parking lot. I said "finally" because the facility was quite a distance from the main high way.

As it went, however, I chose to suppress that funny feeling. My wife and I had thoroughly enjoyed our vacation and I wasn't about to allow a weird and unexplainable feeling to impair my joy. Besides, I was hungry and I looked forward to my upcoming catfish dinner.

Looking back, I don't know what was wrong with me on that yesteryear afternoon. I should have taken stock of my innermost feelings. In addition, there were other things that just were not right! Like, when we entered the place and all eyes shifted to us and, then, slowly glanced elsewhere. And all of those eyes, of course, were replete with white faces.

However, even as the hostess took the initiative to seat us at a table (she, too, was Caucasian), we continued to get intermediate stares from the surrounding patrons. But what got me (and I later kicked myself), it seemed like the entire kitchen staff was coming out and purposely looking our way.

But besides frowning in sheer puzzlement, I said nothing and took it all in stride. Only minutes afterwards, my wife ordered a chicken dinner and I requested my catfish meal.

Sometimes, and especially in the nineties, I was guilty of being "too" logical (and sometimes naive too). I truly believed that normal human beings were incapable of doing despicable, evil-inspired acts to people whom they didn't even know. That, to me, was totally logical, sane and intelligent also! But the key word was normal and it emerged crystal-clear to me that day that normal is directly contrary to racism. In fact, the two terms do not even belong in the same sentence. In a certain sense, they are polar opposites.

In hindsight, I was "stupidly" guilty of overlooking the obvious. I should have never pulled into that restaurant's parking lot and I surely should not have dined inside of it either. After being practically baptized in the fires of racial hatred, I stood convicted of totally under estimating it.

From the moment my wife and I left the restaurant on that rather ominous afternoon, I felt queasy and sick to my stomach. In addition, my head was flush and I was perspiring heavily. That prompted me to ask my wife to drive and I hurriedly climbed into the car's passengers side. "Are you alright?" I asked my wife. "Cause I'm not, and I feel awful."

Thankfully, my lady was doing fine. Seemingly, she had no ill effects whatsoever. But for me, it was an exercise in pure hell! Within five minutes of returning to the interstate, I spotted an

Racism, Sexism, Trumpism, Pseudo-Christianity and the Cinema

upcoming rest area and insisted that my wife rush towards it. And with a look of fret on her face, she did just that.

It was in the nick of time too! Because from the moment the car was pulled into a parking space, I hurriedly disembarked it and started to almost violently throw up. I was, of course, headed for the men's lavatory but I vomited four, different times before even reaching its door, including once in the adjacent flower bed. Then, once inside the men's room, I used the toilet and soon started feeling better.

In fact, after I rinsed my mouth out several times, I was completely free of any ill effects. When I returned to my automobile, I was severely depressed and awash with anger and anxiety. I vented and ranted, talking to my then-relieved wife.

"Those damn honkies did something to my food," I told her. "And whatever it was, it was nasty and downright disgusting! What would drive a person to do that? And how sick and demented could they be? Those mothers don't know me from Adam in the Bible—and, yet, just because of my skin color, they stoop to do something nasty and gross like they did!

How can they bring themselves to look in the mirror? Those dirty, sick, scum-bag sons-of-bitches! "Eventually and shortly, I was able to calm myself. My wife maintained that the person, or persons, who committed the despicable act (and I firmly believed it was a group action) were not even worth getting "hot and bothered" over. She also suggested that such individuals needed sincere prayer.

Admittedly, she was always more religious than I was. I told her I would pray for the "godless skunks" after they die and go to hell—where they so justly belonged. I may sound harsh, but I don't believe there's any salvation for individuals who are void of conscience and are evil-incarnated

Later on, as my outrage subsided, I seriously reflected on that restaurant incident. And I calmly shared it with my wife after I resumed being the designated driver.

"Suppose—just suppose I would have died?" I speculated.

"Suppose the nasty crap they put in my food had taken me away from here? An autopsy would have confirmed that the bastards had poisoned me. You still have the receipt from the restaurant. They would have been in a world of trouble.

You would have hired an attorney, right?"

My wife could not refrain from laughing. "And I would have been a rich woman, right?" she jokingly remarked.

"Aw, boy stop it."

I, too, surrendered to laughter in light of my spouse's response. But till this day, I have never gotten over what occurred at that restaurant. I've played it over and over again in my mind. I've even reviewed the event, reversing the race of the parties involved. In essence, if my wife and I had been a white couple and everyone in the restaurant had been black, would such a vile thing had happened?

I honestly believe the answer would be emphatically "No" and the history of race relations in America practically verifies my belief. One of my chief criticisms of Afro-American people {my people) is that they are almost "too" forgiving and "too" accommodating as well. Take, for instance, the murderous happening involving Dylan Roof. I don't believe if Roof was a black youngster attending a predominantly white church, he would have been greeted with opened arms. I can't be certain, but it wouldn't shock me to learn that those black churchgoers felt honored to have that devil-inspired shooter in their midst. Not because they were so-called "Uncle Toms" or they particularly cherished Caucasian folks either, but because of their Christian faith and upbringing.

As I stated before, I have an insatiable love for people in general. But I must confess that I have a deep-seated affection for fellow black people. And not because of our skin connection, but because I've always been in awe of black America's resilience and optimistic spirit. It, both, amazes me and warms my heart when, in the throes of mourning a murdered loved one, Afro-Americans

Racism, Sexism, Trumpism, Pseudo-Christianity and the Cinema

can step forward and verbally "forgive" the guilty or alleged killer. I think that is uncommonly remarkable!

Now, if I am wrong about my Dylan Roof supposition, then I'm willing to debate it. I can only draw on my personal experiences. Back in Fort Sam Houston in the sixties, when I was the only Negroid soldier in a barracks filled with Caucasian soldiers, I could not stray from the immediate vicinity without having my foot-locker and two wall-lockers turned bottom side up.

Although none of those white soldiers had ever laid eyes on me and didn't know me from the Biblical Adam either, they felt compelled to flex their racist muscles in the hope of dashing my spirits. However, their evil desire was never fully sated. Maintaining an expression of calmness, I simply turned my lockers upright, opened them up and straightened my clothing and, eventually, took to my bunk, reading a book. After behaving in similar fashion for about a week, the locker assaults finally subsided.

To be completely honest, I have never gotten over that 1963 happening and I occasionally reflect back to that restaurant ordeal too. They both remain incomprehensive to me. I am certain those episodes occurred, I was a major player in them but, still, I can't figure them out!

Speaking realistically though, upon dwelling on the discriminatory incidents that transpired inside a Waffle House and a Starbucks earlier this very year, I have to conclude that, "It's the same old soup warmed over," and, sorrowfully, that same pot sits eagerly on the stove.

"Walking in the Shoes of Black Folks"

I'm not sure when it happened but at some point in my life, I stopped thinking about racism per se. I felt it was firmly sewn into the fabric of America and the majority of white folks seemed to embrace and savor it. Apparently, as long as black people didn't infringe on their blessed lives, they found comfort in their privileged world. I, as a person of color, was resolute in co-existing with them and enhancing the lives of my immediate loved ones. I did not cry "uncle" but I came to realize it was all but futile to change white minds.

However, at that same point in time, there was some thing that was practically gnawing at my mind and I could not shake it. Although the average, everyday person might deem it trivial or somewhat asinine (especially Caucasians), I was oftentimes upset and disenchanted with a number of fellow black people. I had interacted with white folks all my life and, therefore, there was nothing they said or did that, after a while, surprised me. Some of their actions were expected and predictable. But when it came to Afro-Americans, individuals who looked like me and were well-acquainted with racial discrimination themselves, I was, sometimes, appalled and mentally unhinged in the presence of their mean-spirited conduct with fellow blacks. If anyone should have been empathetic and sympathetic to the age-old plight of black citizens, it certainly should have been them. And I didn't shy away from letting them know it either.

My half-a-century friendship with Tony is based on sincere affection and mutual respect. It is free of condescension and verbal suppression. Even if we disagree on a topic (and we do), we negotiate a stalemate and walk away with a loving spirit. We realize we're representative of two very different worlds and we occasionally agree to disagree. After all, there's no way Tony can become me and I can't become him. I stated all of the foregoing because I was once in the presence of another black-white alliance, a so-called friendship. And I branded it "so-called" because it was farcical and somewhat shameful in nature. As if I didn't have enough vexations swirling around me when I worked for the St. Louis Police Department in the late 1960's, I was made to deal with, yet, another irritating situation.

Located adjacent to the Prisoner Processing section (my work-

Racism, Sexism, Trumpism, Pseudo-Christianity and the Cinema

site) was the prisoner-intake area (or hold over). It was replete with numerous cells for housing incoming arrestees and especially the ones who were slated to be interviewed and processed. And that happened to be where the two rather obnoxious "friends" worked. One of them was black and the other, white—and of German heritage, and they were both employed as "turnkeys." It was positively uncanny how quickly I came to dislike the pair.

However, that was a complete novelty for me. Up until that time, I identified with Will Rogers. I prided myself at "never meeting a man (or woman) I didn't like" But from the very moment I came into contact with the turnkey duo, that analogy instantly went down the tubes.

I selected the term "contact" because, in reality, I was never formally introduced to either turnkey and my initial exposure to them was essentially auditory. Since the Prisoner Processing section was situated right next to the arrestee in-take area (with only a wall and a steel-bar door betwixt them), it was easy to overhear ongoing conversations, and especially when they were loud and rather agitating. And that was how I felt in the aftermath of the verbal exchange between the two friends on an early Monday morning. For clarification only, I"11 refer to the black fellow as "Ronnie" and his white counterpart as "Hans."

It was obvious that Hans was addressing one or two of his other white co–workers, and not his close-knit black buddy, when he laughingly declared, "Ronnie came over to my house Saturday afternoon! My wife wasn't too happy 'bout it. But she cooked us up a meal, a great meal. But my old lady couldn't help herself. She ain't so hot on Negroes. Soon after Ronnie left out later, she broke up his plate and his drinking glass and tossed 'em both into the trash!"

Amid a round of chuckling, Ronnie opted to issue a response. But instead of coming across as if he was insulted, he, too, sounded somewhat cheerful. "Aw, Hans, you oughta stop that stuff," he laughingly remarked. "You say that all the time. Yo' wife treats me good, really good when I come over there."

"Yeah, she be glad when your butt's gone though," Hans offered, chuckling again. "She's a good actress, that woman of mine." In retrospect, maybe I was being too critical or judgmental. But as time went forward, demeaning conversations similar to the one cited above seemed commonplace between the two turnkey buddies and, to say the least, they managed to get on my last nerves.

Although I kept it to myself, I disliked them both and I was quite sorrowful whenever our work shifts meshed.

To be perfectly frank, my disdain for the Caucasian turnkey, Hans, was not overly tense. I had been exposed to a number of white boys who regarded black people as "clowns" and, in my estimation, he had found one in Ronnie. And I knew, too, if Hans had an authentic friend in his life, he was white like he was

However, when it came to Ronnie, my disenchantment with him rose substantially whenever our paths crossed, and especially when we pulled the same work shift. It wasn't because of something he had said though, and not even because of his subservient behavior around Hans. It was due to something he habitually did, an act that I branded absolutely appalling.

Every town, city, hamlet or what have you, has its share of drunks and derelicts and the city of Saint Louis is no different. Therefore, when I clerked at the Prisoner Processing division in the 60's, I frequently observed a slew of down and out souls being brought into the nearby prisoner intake section. And while most of them were not guilty of committing serious criminal acts, many of them were semi-conscious and incoherent. That was expressly why a couple of wheelchairs were on hand in the section.

Well it goes without saying that the "turnkey" employees were not happy campers when it came to dealing with derelicts and "bums." They constantly scoffed and complained about them,

Racism, Sexism, Trumpism, Pseudo-Christianity and the Cinema

branding them dirty, smelly and drunk out of their minds at times.

But, nevertheless, the majority of the turnkeys were able to suppress their distaste and follow standard procedures. Oftentimes, it merely meant that they would secure the suspect or detainee in one of the wheelchairs and then roll him back to one of the outlying cells. If the person was inebriated, he would be given ample time to sleep it off in their cell.

However, not all of the turnkeys were sticklers for protocol. In fact, one of them was downright ornery and dispassionate. His name happened to be Ronnie and he had an agenda that was totally contrary to all of his fellow co–workers, including his buddy, Hans.

As I indicated, I was already turned off by the rather phony and lopsided-type relationship between Hans and Ronnie. Seemingly, Ronnie was the congenial butt to Hans frequent jokes, and most of them subtly bigoted. As I stated, despite my feelings, I bit my tongue and said nothing. But when I periodically focused on the neighboring prisoner in take area and sighted Ronnie doing something that was, both, unseemly and crude, I could not refrain from speaking out.

This fellow black man (and I felt shame in identifying Ronnie as such) derived some kind of sick pleasure from transporting incoming, semi-conscious derelicts to the out lying cell area. And I deemed it "sick" because, instead of seating the prisoner in a standard wheelchair, Ronnie thought nothing of dragging the men by their two legs. That, naturally, meant the prisoner's head and back were flush with the concrete floor. However, the ugliness of the act escalated even further when it occurred to me that the abused individuals were exclusively black. That was a bridge too far for me and I took it upon myself to voice my protest. In fact, it transpired right in the midst of doing my own job. Even as my officer supervisor, Elliot, was actively fingerprinting a suspect at the time, I stood affront the steel door and verbally blasted Ronnie.

"Why are you dragging that man like that?" I shouted out. "I notice you do that all the time and it's always to a black man! Are all the wheelchairs friggin' broken or something?

What's your damn problem, man?" Highly resentful of my angry remarks, Ronnie was in the middle of telling me to "Mind my own damn business" when the bystanding Elliot entered into the fracas. My supervisor had all the right to scold me for suddenly shifting away from my assigned work task, but he didn't. Instead, he aligned himself with my concerns.

"I've noticed you doing that shit too, Ronnie," he irately spoke, casting his eyes at the turnkey. "And it ain't right, damn it! If I see it again, I'm gonna take you to task for it! Like my clerk said, that's what the goddamn wheel chairs are for. I'm telling you, I don't wanna see the crap no more!"

Essentially, that was the end of Ronnie's demeaning behavior. Owing to a boisterous chastisement and threat from a white man, he obligingly straightened up and flew right after that. Never did I observe seeing him drag an incoming arrestee again, neither a white one or a black one. And upon quitting my job at Prisoner Processing, never again did I lay eyes on the turnkey "friends" either. Thank God for even small favors.

Now, when I painstakingly wrote out my blow-by-blow account of the foregoing scenario, I could not help but wonder if any Caucasian people could remotely identify with my innermost feelings. Basically, it's because white people almost never deal with similar nonsense. For the most part, they are totally oblivious to racial discrimination.

Oh—they might occasionally experience disdain from their Negroid counterparts, but it's usually an outgrowth reaction to white oppression. And, certainly, they haven't encountered fellow white folks who are "pro-black." Personally, I have never, ever met a die-hard black racist. Again, not ever!

In the throes of the commentary above, I'd like to take people (especially, white people) on an imaginary trip. You don't have to pack a bag or a suitcase, you don't have to climb aboard a plane, a

Racism, Sexism, Trumpism, Pseudo-Christianity and the Cinema

train or even an automobile, and you will still be in your personal comfort zone after the make shift trip concludes. It would greatly help, however, if you, as an accommodating traveller, would embark on the journey with an open, empathetic and uncluttered mind. Please indulge me.

As a prerequisite to that impending trip, I'd like to cite the following:

(1) Long ago on a yesteryear evening, as I attended a gala church celebration at one of St. Louis' most beautiful hotels, I found myself on an upward-bound elevator with an elderly white woman. A formal affair awaited me and, therefore, I was dressed in an attractive blue-colored tuxedo. In less than a minute, the old woman looked at me and, with fear in her eyes, backed into the elevator's far right corner. And while doing so, she firmly pressed her purse to her bosom.

I, in turn, didn't miss a beat. Peering at the elderly woman intently, I pressed my left hand on my back pants pocket (securing my wallet) and proceeded to back into the elevator's far left corner. White people never cease to amaze me!

(2) When my eldest son turned 17, I took him to a reputable used car facility, hoping to purchase him his very first automobile. He was excited, as was I, but I was intent on finding a car that would fit my financial budget. Well, after my son had test-driven two cars that had caught his eye, the white salesman (who had cordially waited on us) seemed overjoyed at apprising us of something. Smiling

from ear-to-ear, he said, "I know what you guys want! I've got just the vehicle you want. And I'll give you a great deal on it too!"

Minutes later, the salesman escorted me and my son to the biggest, gas-guzzling Cadillac I had ever laid my eyes on. And, seemingly, our Caucasian salesperson was genuinely surprised (and disappointed) when neither I nor my son was impressed. We soon left that car lot and, alternately, purchased an auto elsewhere. Again I say, white folks never cease to amaze me!

(3) In the summer of 1963, I was a soldier who was stationed in Fort Sam Houston, Texas. In mid-July of that year, my entire company (a mobile army hospital) was air-lifted to South Carolina where we, subsequently, participated in what was regarded as "war games."

When the mock operation concluded a month later, I, along with three of my close-knit army buddies (one of them, black and the other two, white) were on administrative break in downtown Augusta, Georgia. We were all garbed in our standard, dress-khaki uniforms and were planning to attend an afternoon movie. After mild discussion, I eventually persuaded my three comrades to choose "A Gathering of Eagles," starring Rock Hudson. Then, we all approached the ticket booth and laid our fare down. Although the female ticket agent was visually nervous, she soon stated, "I'm sorry, boys–but colored soldiers ain't allowed in this here

Racism, Sexism, Trumpism, Pseudo-Christianity and the Cinema

movie theater. And the one farther up the street neither, I'm afraid. I am so sorry, boys."

Now, there is no need to elaborate on that incident any further. All four of us (incidentally, my friend, Tony, was in that group also) were instantly appalled and taken aback and, to be honest, it's a reminiscence I strongly detest. Notably, in less than a year's time after that happening, a childhood friend of mine was killed in South Vietnam. Of course, he was "colored" and my friend's youthful demise added emphasis to that movie-house memory.

In addition, when I relive that 1963 happening and recall, too, that I was earning a measley $78.00 per month when I enlisted in the service, it further stokes my inner outrage. And I have never gotten over the fact that Negroes were expected and obligated to fight and, maybe, perish in Vietnam but were not allowed to attend a cinema in the deep south. That was a mind-set that was beyond comprehension to me, but, apparently, not for Caucasians.

Therefore, I again declare that white people never, ever cease to amaze me!

At this juncture, I have a confession to make. While I am still determined to take that hypothetical trip I previously proposed, I figuratively tossed in the narratives regarding (1) The elevator, (2) The used automobile and (3) The movie theater to drive home a particular point. I view the trio as "excess baggage" because they are ever-present carry-ons in regards to black travelers. Meaning, even when African Americans are not in the physical presence of Caucasian folks, they are still bedeviled by past racism encounters.

But that's not the end of the picture. Because, unfortunately, and it grieves me to acknowledge this, even when white people are nonentities (indirectly or entirely), black citizens are subjected to discriminatory measures almost daily. Shamefully, the chief executors of such biasness are fellow persons of color. In the black community, we frequently accuse individuals of "tripping" when they behave in such a foul manner. Therefore, it is most appropriate for the reader to join me on my imaginary trip.

(A) There was a time when my wife was in a Saint Louis city hospital, fighting breast cancer. And, simultaneously, my mother was in, yet, another hospital, recuperating from heart-bypass surgery. To report that it was a hectic, difficult period for me is an understatement. After all, my spouse and I still had kids at home and I still worked every day.

Obviously, I had a lot on my plate but I thought I was on top of things. Then again, maybe not. On May 15th (during the year I'm referencing) I was driving en route to my staple work site and, to my surprise, I observed a flashing light behind me. It was emanating from a police car. However, since I had not done anything wrong (I had just executed a left turn and I turned on the proper arrow), I was somewhat irritated.

My irritation persisted as I pulled over and stopped, thereby granting the tailing cop enough space to park behind me. And I still was a bit miffed as I rolled the driver side window down and observed the patrolman approaching my position.

"Officer, why are you stopping me?" I asked, looking to my left. The cop was white and I, therefore, expected a curt response. But he was cordial. "Your license plate is expired," he said.

"It expired in April."

Now I knew I was out of order, but I couldn't believe it! I even disembarked my car, saying, "What? I can't believe this!"

Surprisingly, the officer didn't react. He stood by silent as I proceeded to my car's rear. I was virtually dumbfounded as I viewed my license plate.

"This is shocking!" I remarked. "I've been driving around half a month, and I'm just now getting stopped. Look, officer, my wife is in one hospital and my mother's in another hospital. Plus, I never received a notice from the motor vehicles department about this."

Well, as it turned out, the patrolman was marginally

Racism, Sexism, Trumpism, Pseudo-Christianity and the Cinema

sympathetic. He said he was sorry to hear about my problems, and wished me luck. Then, he issued me a ticket and confiscated my driver's license. I could not justly be upset with him and I took it all in stride. And I was intent upon saying nothing else to the cop until he made a parting remark to me. He told me to "Have a nice day."

I was, then, back behind my steering wheel but I quickly stuck my head out my window. "Officer, can I ask you something?" I yelled. "I'm not trying to be a smart ass or nothing. But when you were in the police academy, and they talked about handing out traffic tickets, did they suggest that you say 'Have a nice day' to people in the aftermath?" The patrolman offered up a sly grin, then said, "Yeah, they do—as a matter of fact." "Uh-huh, sure they did," I replied, starting up my engine.

It's funny how things happen in this life. When the officer issued me that traffic violation ticket on the particular afternoon I referenced, it was after two-thirty P.M. In fact, he wrote 2:47 P.M. on it.

Oddly enough, I left work at 4:35 P.M. (less than two hours after that traffic stop) and on my way home to Berkeley, Missouri, I was pulled over once again by a police officer.

However, since I was driving through a suburban area called University City, my uniformed antagonist was employed by Saint Louis county instead of the city and he was not a white man either. He was, in fact, Afro-American and from the soured expression on his face, I sensed things were not going to go well between us.

Regardless of my snap assumption though, I was intent upon being pleasant myself. I even smiled as I rolled my window down and presented my ticket to the patrolman. "I didn't realize until this afternoon," I offered, "that I was driving around with an expired license plate."

Notably, I didn't receive a return grin from the cop. Instead, he grasped the ticket, said absolutely nothing, and turned and briskly walked back to his vehicle.

Observing him via my rearview mirror, I was sure he was checking if my car was listed as stolen (which was something the other lawman had done earlier) and I dismissed it as procedural. But when the lawman finally returned to my car and asked me something that was ridiculous, I was no longer in a congenial mood.

"Why haven't you had this taken care of?" he grumpily quizzed.

I maintained my calm and issued a reply. "I got that ticket around two-thirty, and that was a little over a couple of hours ago," I explained. "I got off of work at four-thirty. Exactly when did I have the time to take care of it?"

The policeman returned the ticket to me at that juncture, but he wasn't through being difficult. "Ya know–I could issue you a citation," he stated.

I responded, "Well, maybe you could–but why in the hell would you? Because you can?" Of course, my attitude did not please the officer and I didn't really care.

"Well–I'll see your black ass again," the patrolman vowed.

As always, I could not refrain from shaking my head in exasperation. But I wasn't at a loss for words. In response to the cop's foregoing threat, I said, "Not if I see your black ass first!"

I drove off after that but I could not help thinking: Now, he's the officer who should have said, 'Have a nice day.'

(B) When a now-plentiful chicken franchise opened up its first facility in the St. Louis region, I was working at a public high school. The fast-food franchise was already extremely popular in other cities and states and, therefore, when it came to the "Lou," it already had a built-in fanbase. I, along with the school's head custodian and a number of teachers, were a part of that select fan base and we came together one morning with a desire to sate our craving. Simply stated, we pooled our monies together and looked forward to having fried chicken for lunch.

While our teacher cohorts busily taught their respective classes,

Racism, Sexism, Trumpism, Pseudo-Christianity and the Cinema

I and my custodian friend boarded my car and made our way to the newly-opened facility. It was located approximately thirty minutes away from the school itself and since the lunch hour officially commenced at 12:15 P.M. my comrade and I headed out at 11:00 A.M.

Thankfully, the place was not crowded on the morning I'm recollecting. Actually, in addition to two other customers, there was a couple of cooks, a cashier and a manager. Incidentally, the work crew was behind the counter and everyone in the place happened to be black. My cohort and I put our order in, forty-two pieces of chicken and several side dishes, and the bill totaled up to almost seventy dollars. But not too long after receiving the paper bill and the left over change, things went awry.

My custodian friend, being fully aware of the impending trip back to our work place, opted to make a request. Upon observing the freshly fried chicken pieces being poured into the bin, he pleasantly spoke to the female cashier. "

Excuse me, young lady," he spoke. "Look—We got a long way to go. So can you give us the chicken that's just comin' outta the frier?"

For reasons I could not at all understand, the cashier rolled her eyes at my comrade and then started to rather begrudgingly throwing the piping-hot chicken pieces into two large containers. (If body language could kill, my friend would have died on the spot). Then, when she set the chicken boxes on the counter, next to our bagged complement items, she decided to add insult to injury. Out of the clear blue sky, she stared at my comrade, saying, "I hope it burns the roof of your mother fucking mouth!" My custodian friend was visually stunned and cluelessly looked towards me, asking, "What brought that on? What? what did I say wrong?"

In actuality, my buddy didn't have to say anything else. I took it from there. I leveled a verbal blast on that brazen cashier that I was sure she'd long remember. I was so infuriated and boisterous, in fact, the manager came rushing forward.

"What's the matter, Sir?" he asked me. "I mean–what the devil is going on here?"

With a face of anger, I calmed myself and looked toward the rather subdued and now-silent young woman. "We've got a distance to go with our order," I explained to the manager.

"My friend, here, asked her nicely to give us the chicken that had just come up. And you know what she told him?

She said 'I hope it burns the roof of your m-f mouth!' And she didn't say m-f either."

The manager faced his cashier in total disbelief. Frowningly, he questioned, "You didn't say that, did you, Alicia?"

I wasn't quite finished. "Yeah, she said it," I insisted. "And you should have seen her face. But, you know what? I betcha she wouldn't have said that to a damn white customer. Naw, that's the kind of disrespect you show to only fellow black folks."

The manager stood, shaking his head in sheer dismay. "Could you give me your receipt, please?" he asked my nearby friend.

At that point, the somber manager grasped the receipt and proceeded over to the cash register. He, then, refunded our money in its entirety, telling us our order was free and apologized on behalf of his very rude employee. He also vowed, "I'll take care of her" as my comrade and I walked out the door. Despite our order being free, it was a long time before either of us revisited that fast-food facility.

(C)As a young man, I was an avid reader and one of the books I read was "Invisible Man" (not the one by H.G. Wells, but the one by Ralph Ellison). It was written by a black man and it was a profound commentary on how people of color are generally viewed by far too many white folks in this world. Hence, like the book's title suggests, black people are, oftentimes, non-entities to the

Racism, Sexism, Trumpism, Pseudo-Christianity and the Cinema

majority of whites. In a certain sense, blacks, or Afro-Americans, are truly invisible to them.

However, that hypothesis was never surprising or newsworthy to me. Even before I laid eyes on Ellison's book, I had long concluded that, for the most part, Caucasian people could not see Afro-American people. As I suggested priorly, white folks remain in their comfort zones, wearing blinders and they choose not to see pass their noses. That mind-set is vital to their presumed feeling of superiority and it always has been.

I know it comes across as repetitive, but I am no longer shocked by anything Caucasian people do (from church bombings and school shootings to over-aggressive cops and even gerrymandering and voter suppression) but it bothers the hell out of me when fellow black citizens emerge as irritant satellites to white folks.

For instance, I was in a St. Louis county department store about ten years ago. I had picked out two shirts and I was standing in line, waiting to pay for them. It seemed like I was standing there for an hour (mainly because the female cashier, who was black, was engaged in a prolonged conversation with the white woman at her counter), but, admittedly, I was never a patient shopper anyhow. I have never been fond of shopping.

Finally, the chatty cashier bidded goodbye to the departing customer and took a few steps towards me. (By that time, there were other waiting shoppers standing near me)

However, instead of addressing me, she instantly established eye-contact with the Caucasian man behind me.

Smilingly, she asked him, "May I help you, sir?

Right away, I announced, "No, you can help me."

"Well, I didn't know who was next," the cashier snapped, obviously offended.

"Well—evidently you can talk," I retorted, "and you could just as well have asked, 'Who's next.' That would have cut down on any confusion."

"Aw–you just wanna be difficult," the young cashier argued in the middle of grasping my shirts. "I don't have time for this."

As usual, I wasn't at a loss for words "Neither do I, young lady. I just like being waited on whenever my turn comes around. Every person does," I stated.

Frankly, it wouldn't surprise me one iota if some of the readers of the foregoing account (essentially, Caucasians) opt to brand me "difficult" or even "overly sensitive," but they would be way off the mark. (It's simply because they, in their white skin, are hardly ever, if ever, subjected to similar, unprovoked slights). I once dealt with a black fast-food worker who was grinning and joking with the white patron in front of me and then turned around, completely void of her previous smile, and addressed me, asking, "Yeah–what do you want?"

And that's not the worst case scenario. I went to the St. Louis Teacher's Credit Union one afternoon (which was something I did on weeks when I didn't get paid) and endured an 'out of the blue' insult from the black clerk behind the counter.

After I stood in line, calmly awaiting my turn, the clerk (who happened to be female) nastily remarked, "Every time I look up, you're coming in here for some damn money!"

I was instantly taken aback. I actually couldn't believe she was addressing me. I even pointed to my chest, making eye-contact with the lady and I questioned, "Are you talking to me?"

Believe it or not, I wasn't thinking about Robert De Niro at that time (from the film 'Taxi Driver) but when I reflected back later on, I had to acknowledge that I must have sounded like him.

"Yeah–I'm talking to you," the lady boldly owned up to her words.

Now, I had seen the woman before but I never had had a single conversation with her. Therefore, I didn't know what her problem was. "Miss, I don't know where you're coming from," I spoke. "But if it bothers you so much to look up-damnit, then don't look up! I'm here to get money that's taken out of my paycheck! And if I

Racism, Sexism, Trumpism, Pseudo-Christianity and the Cinema

come in here every hour on the hour, it's your damn job to give me my money! And I don't give a flying crap if you keep your stupid head down! Stop looking up! What the Sam hell is your problem anyhow?"

At that precise juncture, the credit union's general manager (a white man) emerged from his nearby office. He, of course, had heard my boisterous rant and he immediately tried to calm me down.

Then, as the lady clerk remained quiet and looked embarrassingly at her interceding supervisor, he offered me an apology. I, eventually, accepted it, the manager personally issued me my requested money, and I soon departed the facility. Regretfully, I never found out why that clerk behaved in the manner she did. In addition, I never saw her again either.

I am quite positive that some of the readers of my stories about racist whites and self-loathing blacks will be regarded as trivial and somewhat asinine as well. Plus,

I am aware that a segment of people will find them difficult to believe, to some degree, exaggerative and even absurd. But I painstakingly relived them with a lingering measure of hope in my heart. I embarked on that imaginary trip, inviting others to join me, sincerely praying that people take out time and seriously rethink racism and its far-reaching effects.

As I professed several times earlier, I have always been an avid movie buff. And when I reflect on the film "To Kill a Mockingbird," which starred Gregory Peck as a lawyer named Atticus Finch, I see great merit in something the wise attorney (and father)–told his two children. He said (and, again, I'm paraphrasing)" You never know a man until you have stood in his shoes and walked around in them." Sadly, despite my optimism and my ever-present hopefulness, that seems to be a bridge much too far regarding John Q. Public–in spite of their racial identities. The hatred inspired merry-go-round continues to revolve and, tragically, it exhibits no sign of halting or even slowing down.

Sexism

"Throughout my entire life time, there are two beings I have never laid my eyes on. I have never seen an alien from another planet—and I've never seen an American husband who can digest the meal of infidelity he frequently serves his wife. Not ever."

Man Should Not Live By Bed Alone

In the late 1960's when I engaged in a one-on-one meeting with Saint Louis city's Chief of Police, I frankly told him that, "Everything in this country, Sir, has to do with race." I sat in front of the man, protesting the racist actions of two of his over-zealous white officers and he, essentially, dismissed my concerns. The Chief, like far too many Caucasians I've interacted with, was in a state of denial and a mendacity mode.

However, I wholeheartedly believe there's verifiable truism in what I said about race, then and at present, and I am prepared to make my case. Sexism in America cannot be honestly discussed without travelling back in time; back to an era when sex itself was exploitatious and self-serving. That time was called "slavery" and although it is now considered despicable and unlawful too, its affect lingers on.

Although black men no longer function as studhorses and supplanted fathers (a premise that increased the wealth of Caucasian slave-owners), the psychological damage that was rooted in that cruel, inhumane system has never been fully addressed.

Racism, Sexism, Trumpism, Pseudo-Christianity and the Cinema

Tragically, and somewhat unknowingly, there is a large segment of Afro-American men in this country who have embraced and perpetuated that slave-time mentality.

But the fault does not rest solely on the backs of unsophisticated black men. Even as white people stand back and point fingers of blame, verbally criticizing black citizens for every misstep they make, they must shoulder a portion of the fault. In their safe and privileged havens they may cry, "Slavery is over, so get over it" or "I wasn't even alive during slavery, so I can't be held accountable for it," but those comments are froth with naivety and blatant ignorance.

If Caucasians were fortunate enough to inherit wealth and property from their yesteryear ancestors, then it is most appropriate that they inherit their well-documented wrongdoings and age-old sins also. Grievously, while those sins were exempt from punishment or even marginal repercussions, they have taken a catastrophic toll on the black community.

History records that the "Emancipation Proclamation" prohibited slavery in America, but it entirely skirted over the enduring and devastating damage it did to the black psyche.

There were no trained or empathetic counselors around and no organized effort to help or assist former slaves as they transitioned to so-called "freemen." No comforting, no deprogramming or even a glint of human compassion. Absolutely nothing in the offing– except an upsurge in white terrorism and murderous actions which were designed to bedevil former slaves. (Even "forty acres and a mule" was a farcical joke).

For centuries, black men were not only treated like beasts of burden; laboring from sun up until sundown, they were made to be mass breeders also. And in that subservient and demeaning role, they extracted (or "contracted") a sick by-product that festers in the Afro-American community till this very day. Because they were practically emasculated in their lowly status as slaves, many black men took pride in their virility and sexual potence.

Therefore, since there has never been a sustained or concentrated movement to alter or denounce that self-concocted mind-set, it still lives and breathes in modern times. Sorrowfully, there are an inordinate number of Afro-American men who have bought into that rather foolhardy belief. In essence, they have come to measure their manhood in terms of fathering children. And, unfortunately, that is an entrenched and long-standing pox on the black community at-large.

I am fully aware that I'm stepping on the toes of many people who look like me, individuals who walk around with the same skin color I adorn, but the truth cannot be discarded or "crushed to earth." It is one thing to emerge puffed up in the wake of your ability to impregnate one, two or even multiple women, but it's another thing to ignore, disregard or abandon the sum products of those assorted sexual liaisons which, of course, are flesh and blood children.

During slavery time, when black males were subjugated as sperm donors, fathers were oftentimes cruelly and callously separated from their biological offspring's, but that practice no longer exists. Far too many black fathers, and especially youthful ones, seem to choose to be estranged from their children.

However, that charge cannot be solely attributed to young black fathers. A good many of them are impressionable satellites of older black males, sometimes their own fathers. I wish I had a dollar for all of my fellow Afro-American men who spoke to me over the years, pompously boasting of their prowess at producing kids. Seemingly, they wallow in self-adoration, but seldomly expound on what's in store for their newly-born offsprings. And so many times, since a number of those braggadocios individuals are, in fact, already married, the immediate future for those subject children looks rather bleak. Furthermore, if you, as the on-hand listener, is acutely aware that the braggart is barely taking care of his immediate family, it is downright shameful and depressing.

To my utter regret, I was once exposed to an older black man

Racism, Sexism, Trumpism, Pseudo-Christianity and the Cinema

who was totally ridiculous. He took great pride and joy in fathering two different children on the very same day.

He smilingly announced, "I know I'm a hell'uva man. My wife and my girlfriend gave birth to my two babies on the same damn day, in the same hospital and on the same maternity ward. One was a boy and the other, a girl but I wonder do that make them twins? Whatchu think?"

As I stated previously, I have never been one to mince my words. Plus, I'm somewhat candid. "Naw, that in no way makes those babies twins," I asserted" but it does make them both unlucky. After all, look who they drew as a father, you."

Of course, it goes without saying that my boasting associate did not much care for my comment but I never regretted making it. I only wish I had personally been on hand when I was apprised of similar ridiculous and damning declarations. One of my childhood chums, a fellow who had fathered four kids by three different women, once informed me of the advice he and his brothers had been given by their dad.

"My old man always told us," he grinningly informed me, "That if you git a chance to git a piece, then knock it outta the box. Tear it up!"

I was practically dumbfounded that day and somewhat subdued too. I withheld my tongue though.

After all, I realized my friend dearly loved his dad and I did not wish to rain on his parade. However, when I took time to seriously ponder my comrade's "fatherly" advice, I wondered if his dad ever regretted his sexual endorsement. Just like me, my friend's dad was well aware of his son's financial woes. The father knew my friend (his son) was married with a teenaged son of his own and realized, too, that his son was paying child support for three outside children.

That was a tough financial row to hoe but when you focus on the trio of kids who were obliged to deal with a part-time and, essentially, absent father, it was truly heartbreaking. In my personal

67

estimation, it would bold well for responsible parents (fathers and mothers too) to share that part of the equation with their children. That would be advice well worth while.

Several years ago, when I worked part-time as a school bus driver, one of my male co–workers was fed up with the mean-spirited and disrespectful teenagers who regularly rode his bus. Throwing up his hands in frustration, he asked, "What the hell is the matter with the young people of today?"

In less than a moment's passing, I responded with an assessment I've long clinged to. I said, "Believe it or not, they've been exposed to too many old men from yesterday.

So many of those kids are fatherless, they feel abandoned and they are pissed off at the whole world. A lot of them have gotten a raw deal. And they surely were not born the way they are."

Naturally, I'm not anti-older people (hell, I'm old myself) but when I look back and recall grown and elderly individuals touting their sexual prowess in the presence of younger men, it raises my dander. When I hear them crowing, boldly patting themselves on their backs for fathering a batch of kids (never mind that they don't take time to raise them), it makes me furious. I'm tempted to admonish them (and I have in several instances), remind them that they are not doing anything that a dog in the street can't do. I'd tell them that if you're going to spew out unsolicited advice to youngsters, then tell them something that will help them in the future and not harm or hinder them.

When it comes to young people, middle-aged and elderly men have so many life experiences to share. And they do not all involve sex and procreation either. For instance, men of color could apprise younger Afro-Americans that solely due to their black skin, they are born behind the eight ball. Since they are so wise, maybe they could tell youths how to sidestep or distance themselves from that figurative eight ball. Or, upon informing black youths that they are made to play against a stacked deck, they could possibly caution them not to play too many card games with white folks.

Racism, Sexism, Trumpism, Pseudo-Christianity and the Cinema

In essence, in no uncertain terms, without mincing their words, they could tell young black people "what's up." Just like Will Smith's character kept repeating in the movie "Concussion," tell them "the truth." Tell them the importance of getting an education (finish high school and try college), tell them to avoid jail and prison; stay entirely away from criminal activity.

Tell them not to get dishonorably discharged from the military service. And it is quite important, also, that seasoned black men (and women too) try to school young Afro-Americans in regards to the work world that awaits them. They (we) must inform black youngsters that, although racial discrimination is no longer legal in the United States, there are still mechanisms in place to keep them at bay. Take the initiative to alert those newly black employees that they will always be in competition with their white counterparts (or co-workers) and they should guard against allowing their employers (who are predominantly Caucasian) to build a book on them. Significantly, that book references every misstep and infraction an employee has ever made, and especially when dealing with Afro-American workers.

Now, it wouldn't surprise me that in the wake of my foregoing tirade, I am accused of being anti-white or even a racist myself but I am hell-bent on keeping it "real." I am expounding on something that will benefit the well-being of all people of color, not only black folks. Unfortunately, we still live in an unjust, color-conscious world, a resurging racist world (thanks to our current president) and it saddens me to say that the American condition is worsening with the passing of each day. Therefore, I still maintain that "Everything in this country has to do with race."

However, before I press forward, I'd like to readdress my fellow black men, and especially the ones who are not as elderly as I am. I wish to suggest to them, if you are bent on imparting your "wisdom" on the younger generation (especially the male gender)– please tell them about the backside of their sexual folly. Tell them about the penalties and hassles for not paying child support, tell them about resentful and rebellious outside children, tell them about begrudging so-called "baby mommas" who use their out-of-wed-lock kids as innocent pawns, tell them about youngsters who grow up resenting and, sometimes, hating their dads and their meager living circumstances as well.

And tell them, too, if it's heartfelt in you, that you dearly love and cherish them. Because at the end of the day, that's what matters to a child, not a bunch of apologies or words of regret. And for God's sake, implore your offsprings (if you happen to be part of the problem) not to follow in your poor example. We, as African American people, must break the vicious circle! What good is obtaining physical freedom when we are still mentally shackled in the chains of age-old slavery?

After the foregoing commentary, I am sure there's a segment of fellow United States citizens who will loudly give me their "Amens," and especially white folks sitting on the sideline. But they have a myriad of problems themselves.

When young white boys and men continually go on murderous rampages, there is something rotten in Denmark. Black people come into this world, fighting a steep, uphill battle.

Black youths in America's inner cities seem to be at war with one another. Many of them are poverty-strickened, money-craving, drug-driven and virtually mad at the world. So many of them are fatherless, forlorn and sour on life; overwhelming maladies that seem to follow them day in and day out. But what on earth has gone awry with Caucasian people of unearned privilege, especially the young ones? Why are they so volatile and dangerous?

Admittedly, I do not have a pat answer to those questions, I wish I did, but I do know one thing: Parents, and I'm not singling out only white ones, are no longer fulfilling their God-granted roles. They appear to be habitually saying, "Do as I say" instead of, "Do as I do."

Plainly speaking, hypocrisy has not only caught up with many of us, it has overtaken us. It occurs to me that children (mostly

Racism, Sexism, Trumpism, Pseudo-Christianity and the Cinema

teenagers) are now running America's households while parents are, well, "running around in it."

For example, how can a weapons arsenal exist in a suburbian house and the residing adults, who are called parents, be totally unaware of it? That's unimaginable to me!

Admittedly, I don't know what goes on in white homes across America but something is seriously out of kilter. Maybe Caucasian people are guilty of rationalizing regarding their offspring (believing they are normal when they are not) or they are notoriously slow to act. And, maybe, too, white parents are overly-accommodating when it comes to dealing with their kids. Point being: If you, as a parent or legal guardian, willingly allows your child to "post" you out of specific areas in your house (their bedroom, basements, attics, etc.) then you are subject to be complicit in whatever misdeed or foolishness they engage in.

And if your kid audaciously chides you for infringing on his or her privacy, then "lovingly" encourage them to find a good-paying job, move to a place of their very own and strict privacy will be in the offing. You might denounce me as overly harsh (accuse me of not loving your child), but it beats feeling forever regretful and guilty for the rest of your days.

At some points in life we, as adults, have to make some hard choices whether they involve our children, our spouses, our friends and relatives or individuals we interact with on a daily basis. You give and take, take and give and sometimes you have to say, "Enough is enough." And that's how I view the modern "Me-Too" movement. Men, in general, have been behaving like sexual barbarians and predators for so long and going totally unchecked in the wake of them, that they came to view their actions as "normal" and "acceptable." But they were wrong, dead wrong and women finally decided to mimic the words of Peter Finch in the movie "Network." At long last, they are collectively yelling, "I'm mad as hell and I'm not gonna take it anymore!"

Lionel Barry Harris

Even as a man myself, I have to admit that that outcry is resounding and long overdue. However, in a different viewpoint, I am obliged to withhold my applause. If that movement had prevailed decades ago, American prisons would be overflowing with male sex offenders. In my estimation, men were more provocative and predacious in the past than they are today. And upon making that assertion, I can't help thinking about the following account:

As I indicated previously, there was a time when I worked at a public high school in St. Louis, Missouri. I had my own second-floor office and I enjoyed interacting with a hodgepodge of co-workers and teen-aged students as well. Some of my co-workers; I considered friends. And the lady involved in the incident I'm on the verge of reliving was one of my dearest friends.

In addition to handling school finances, my job agenda consisted of procuring textbooks and a whole gamut of supplies and aids that enhanced the daily educational process. Therefore, as a courtesy to faculty and staff members, I kept the more frequently used supplies at arm's-reach. Behind my desk and swivel chair were shelves filled with various items.

However, on the day I'm recapping, my lady friend did not stop by to retrieve a supply item. She casually bypassed my Dutch door, stood in front of my desk (I was sitting in my chair) and struck up a casual conversation. Whatever we talked about on that particular day, I recall both of us laughing several times.

To give this remembrance a certain texture, I am compelled to mention that my friend and visitor was quite attractive. She had a cute face, she was always well-groomed, always dressed immaculately and was also very shapely. In many quarters, she would have been considered "stacked." However, even in my personal heyday, I would have deemed her a close-knit comrade and clearly off-limits to me. She seemed to be happily married (I even knew her husband) and was a young mother also.

Keeping all of the foregoing in mind, my story actively resumes with, yet, another teacher stepping inside my office. However, he was an older male (certainly older than me and my conversing friend) and since his classroom was located three doors down from my office, I would periodically see him throughout the work day. He and I also enjoyed a congenial relationship. In fact, I had taken the initiative to donate blood for his hospitalized mother a few months back. Therefore, I was fond of him.

As I stated earlier, I had a Dutch door (a half door) and traditionally people (adults and students alike) would stand in the hallway, look in at me and verbally convey their desires. If they were in the hunt for textbooks, supply items, etc., they would utter their request from that corridor vantage point. Like I said, my woman friend was there basically to shoot the breeze.

From the very "git-go," my newly-arrived co-worker was behaving oddly. Although my lady comrade was continually talking, I warily shifted my eyes to the newcomer. But, in return, he wasn't even looking at me. Instead, he was solidly focused on my female visitor. Then, in the passing of a single moment, without uttering a mere word, his focus plunged downward to lustful fixation. My lady friend happened to be wearing a zip-down sweater that day and this bold low-life reached over and swiftly zipped it down!

I saw it with my own eyes, but I couldn't believe I saw it! (I looked like Rod Steiger in the movie "In the Heat of the Night" when Sidney Poitier slapped that wealthy white man back) I was visually stunned and momentarily speechless!

But the same did not apply to my violated female visitor. She was livid and infuriated! Even as she rapidly re-zipped her sweater, she called her molester (and that is exactly what he was) every foul name she could think of. And not only that, she threatened to tell her husband about the weird ordeal, promising the elderly and veteran teacher that her spouse would come up to the school and, "Kick his old, perverted ass!"

Even as my lady co–worker was bawling her assailant out, the man was offering up a makeshift apology. I labeled it "makeshift" because it seemed fake and insincere to me.

He was claiming he was sorry, but he really wasn't. It was more like "The devil made me do it" excuse. And when he soon retreated to his down-the-hall classroom, thereby leaving me and my lady visitor in my office, we both concluded that he wasn't regretful of his actions at all. He may have been sorry for being subjected to the resultant tongue-lashing, but that, to us, was really about it.

And it would have been "it," if the perpetrator of that sexual offense had left it alone and had kept it under wraps. I had told my violated comrade that I would back her all the way–if she elected to file a formal complaint regarding the episode, but she declined, saying she didn't want to wreck the man's career and life. I was somewhat sympathetic too.

As I stated earlier, I liked the teacher who was involved also. But since I was eyewitness to it all, I would be obligated to tell the truth.

However, as I indicated, the elderly teacher would not allow the matter to die down or to normalize. A couple of hours later, my victimized friend returned to my office and she as just as upset as she was earlier. As she handed me a written note, she said, "That bastard is seriously sick! Take a look at this mess."

I took the note and I read it. It stated, 'Please forgive me for what happened in Mr. H's office this morning, but you were looking so good, I couldn't help myself. Again, I'm sorry.'

"He is sick," I frowningly replied, "and stupid too.

He even signed his damn name. What's wrong with him?" Of course, my female friend could not answer my query. She was as baffled regarding the old teacher's behavior as I was. Apparently, he was a long-time sexual predator who was void of remorse. And in my estimation, there was little hope for him.

Now, if you think that's the end of my story, then you are sadly mistaken. About an hour after my friend presented me with the

Racism, Sexism, Trumpism, Pseudo-Christianity and the Cinema

initial note, she returned to my office with, yet, another one. It simply read,

"Again, I humbly apologize for what happened in Mr. H's office this morning.

But—you know a man's going to be a man. Sorry."

In retrospect, I wish I had begged or implored my "female" friend to take my "male" friend to task for his deplorable conduct inside my office. And it wasn't because I chose to loathe the man in the immediate aftermath of the happening (although I was silently miffed at him afterwards) it was due to the behavior (or misbehavior) he displayed during the following weeks.

Not only did I personally observe him doing things that were unbecoming for a teacher and an adult man as well, I frequently overheard a number of shocking remarks that were made by female students. As they congregated in the corridor outside my office, the applicable teenaged girls pulled no punches as they complained about their so-called teacher whom I'll call "Mr. D."

For instance, one afternoon as I sat at my desk, working on the school budget, I heard two girls conversing with each other. I wasn't eavesdropping and neither young lady was purposely near my door way, but their discussion was so loud, I had no trouble hearing them.

Talking in a matter-of-factly manner, one of them declared, "Girl, I know I better git an 'A' in Mr. D's class, the way he be patting me on my ass."

"Me too, girl," responded the second young girl.

"He be grabbing' on me too. Sometimes, I wanna slap his face.

Shit! He better give me a goddamn 'A' or at least a 'B.' I don't wanna have to snitch on his old, nasty ass."

To be candid, the foregoing was just a small sampling of the various criticisms aimed at Mr. D. I overheard other complaints but the girls involved in those episodes we're not so mercenary. They did not equate a stellar grade with a subdued toleration of a lewd act.

Lionel Barry Harris

As I stated before, my personal disenchantment with Mr. D was not solely based on the unsettling remarks made by teenaged girls in the vicinity of my office. I was eyewitness to a few acts that added to my disgust.

Since my office was situated on the second floor and Mr. D's not too distant classroom was located next to the stairwell area, I frequently passed by the seasoned teacher's classroom whenever I elected to go downstairs. The first floor was where the Main Office, the Principal's Office and the school's cafeteria was located. And, sometimes, while casually strolling towards the staircase area, I observed a tell-tale scene on several different occasions. Looking to my left extreme and glancing inside Mr. D's opened-door room, I saw the teacher actively passing out papers to his students.

On the surface, there was nothing strange or out of the ordinary going on. But since it was the era of the mini-skirt and two well-endowed teenaged girls happened to be occupying the front seats in the first two rows, the scene took on a different connotation. The teasing young ladies opened their legs widely just as Mr. D "accidentally" dropped some of his papers and stooped down to retrieve them. Just so happened, too, Mr. D's eyes were fixated on the mini-skirt wearing girls.

Now, that account may sound somewhat amusing to some folks. But to me it was disgusting and unsavory when I witnessed it and it's disgusting and unsavory at present. And if it tickles someone's funny bone, suppose your own daughter was subjected to such shenanigans?

Admittedly, I recounted the story about my female friend and the "zipper" incident because I wanted to say something about the "Me-Too" movement. The antagonist in that story was Mr. D, the elder teacher who couldn't control his sexual impulses. But intelligent people should not buy into that flimsy excuse. Mr. D knew exactly what he was doing.

And he figured, too, that his female victim (my friend) would eventually give him a pass on it. He knew she would not hold

Racism, Sexism, Trumpism, Pseudo-Christianity and the Cinema

him accountable because–he was a married man, because he had children of his very own, and because–he was a career and tenured teacher. In short, Mr. D knew (counted on it, in fact) that his female victim didn't want to be seen as the villain in the matter.

However, the foregoing was only surface stuff. The meat of Mr. D's outlandish conduct lies in the afterthought notes he submitted to his victim. Take the first note, for example. In it, Mr. D said, 'You were looking so good, I couldn't help myself.' In reality, he was simply implying that what he did was practically her fault. In essence, she should not have been "looking so good." Therefore, he was the real victim, not her!

Then came the follow-up note. Throughout my rather lengthy life, I have been in the company of men who seemed to have had no moral compass. When it came to sexual dallying, those men (the single ones and the married ones) flew by the seats of their pants. Many of them had no qualms about jumping into the sack with one woman after another. I may come across as a male prude, but I'm not. I say "to each his own" and the "wrongdoing you do–comes back to you." However, my personal feelings are purely irrelevant. But when I reflect back to Mr. D's second note, I cannot refrain from thinking about men who constantly "allowed their small heads to overrule their big heads."

Now, that may sound rather crude to some people.

But when I dwell on the men I described above, and Mr. D, and think about their shared and patented commonality, I deem their rationale crude also. Almost invariably, they proudly invoke, "A man's gonna be a man," and that, in my estimation, acutely translates to, "A dog is gonna be a dog." I perceive it as a caveman mentality and Mr. D (among others) was an individual who embraced that asinine, abrasive thought pattern.

The bottom line is this: My co-worker, Mr. D, and men of his particular ilk, should never be in a classroom, teaching impressionable children. And I'm not singling out girls, I mean boys also. When young men glimpse their grown, male teacher inappropriately touch female classmates, what signal is being sent to them? When those cited girls were enticingly opening up their legs for Mr. D, what was it telling onlooking boys? Were they wondering–Is this what womanhood is all about? Therefore, Mr. D was detrimental to the normal growth of all students, regardless of their gender.

However, don't think I restrict my critical views to fellow men. Many males are "bad actors" but they do not have a lock on immorality or rationalization either. Quite a number of women are notorious bad players as well. Some of them go through life, trying to force square pegs into round holes also. Meaning, when assorted women engage in sexual wrongdoing, they desperately try to justify their actions too. I call it a "Soap opera mentality" because their behaviours are oftentimes commonplace on daytime television programming.

Like, when some women hook up with married men, they say such things as, "His wife was mistreating him, or doesn't understand him" or "He loves me and he never really loved his wife" or even "His wife doesn't know what to sexually do in the bed with him. And, sometimes, the mistress comes to regard herself as her married suitor's "soulmate." And that, I do not understand at all. When a person tosses the term soul into the discussion, I automatically think about Christianity and God. After all, S-O-U-L is a biblical term.

Therefore, when the outside girlfriend perceives herself as a vital part of that pairing, is she actually suggesting that God inadvertently (or mistakenly) gave her preordained mate to another woman (who happens to be her man's current spouse) first? I'm fully aware that people are adept at making their mouths say anything, but he or she cannot justify wrongdoing by giving it an alternate slant. Maybe, they're referring to "sole" mate, spelled s-o-l-e, though.

Unfortunately, I have been in the presence of dallying men who treat their outside women like lowly footstools, so maybe that's the

Racism, Sexism, Trumpism, Pseudo-Christianity and the Cinema

context they're alluding to. But despite the rationale they ascribe to, the so-called "other woman" usually gets the boot in the final analysis. And in that particular vein, they could be regarded as sole mates after all.

However, no matter what I or anyone else says, women will continue to subject themselves to the, oftentimes, demeaning role of "mistress" or "outside woman." As long as men elect to be unfaithful to their wives, numerous women stand ready to accommodate them. It's a behavior pattern that can be traced all the way back to "David and Bathsheba" in the Holy Bible and there's no sign of it stopping.

Although I strongly denounce extramarital behavior, it is widespread and considered almost normal–by mostly womankind. Married women have dealt with it time and time again throughout the duration of their marital union. To their credit, I have even known wives who have not only accepted their husband's out-of-wedlock babies, but have taken some of those babies into their own households. That's commendable and remarkable. But there's two beings I've never seen in my lengthy life. I have never seen an alien from another planet and I've never met an American husband who can deal with similar crap that they serve up to their spouses. Hardly ever do men come to grips with the infidelity of their wives. And to that I say, 'What's good for the gander is good for the goose.'

There's a particular paradox I've struggled with all my life and it endures to this very day. Over the years, I have constantly asked myself, "Why do individuals who boldly and willingly engage in assorted wrongdoing–think they should come out on top? Why do they, operating in a devil may care mode, expect to be eventually blessed in the wake of their adverse conduct?"

For instance, I once knew a young woman who, upon learning that her spouse was cheating on her, took measures to locate and "have it out" with the so-called home wrecker. "She methodically took the initiative to track down her husband's outside woman and, in person, angrily confronted her.

Spewing out a barrage of profane language and threatening to do bodily harm to her competitor too, she dispensed her aggression while her spouse stood by, looking benign and as innocent as the day was long. However, she said absolutely nothing to her onlooking mate.

Now, you may have no sympathy whatsoever for the admonished other woman in that episode, and you might emerge contemptuous of the bystanding husband as well, but here's the kicker in the matter, the real gist of my account. In that particular case (and in a lot of other cases also), the infuriated wife (the same woman who opted to level that vocal blast on the other woman) had once wittingly played the mistress role herself. She, in fact, was the disparaged "outside woman" prior to marrying her current husband. That, to me, is vintage hypocrisy!

But hypocrisy is prevalent in the "Me-Too" movement also and much of that hypocrisy is affiliated with race and racism. Sure, a number of white men like Charlie Rose, Al Franken, Matt Lauer, Harvey Weinstein, Roger Ales and even Kevin Spacey are casualties of that surging movement but well prior to its advent, black citizens were made to deal with unrelenting biasness. I repeat–"Everything in this country has to do with race."

Take, for example, the well-publicized O.J. Simpson murder case in the 1990's. From the very beginning, I personally believed Simpson was guilty, and I still do.

But I was never fascinated by the happening. It was essentially non-important to me. The "juice", as Simpson was sometimes called, never wanted to be black and, after a while, I didn't want him to be black either. And since I was never a big fan of football anyway, Simpson was a nonentity to me.

But what did intrigue me, what peaked my interest was how Caucasian people behaved or reacted throughout the entire ordeal, and especially when it came to the trial. At that time, I was still employed by the St. Louis Board of Education, still working at the high school level but was, then, situated in a newly-constructed,

Racism, Sexism, Trumpism, Pseudo-Christianity and the Cinema

state-of-the-art learning institution. My co-workers and the enrolled student body took great pride in being at a "college preparatory" high school.

The majority of my fellow employees were white and, for some reason, many of them were not only fascinated by the Simpson murder trial, they were practically obsessed with it. In fact, when the trial finally concluded and the jury was "still out," it would not have surprised me to have learned that the Caucasian teachers could not fully concentrate on their instructing roles.

However, when the bough finally broke, meaning when O.J. Simpson was officially found to be "not guilty" of the double-murders, there was an outcry of rage emanating from those white teachers that was almost indescribable. As my dear mom used to say, "They were mad as a hatter!" I mean, they were visually furious!

In fact, one of the Caucasian female teachers was so upset and beside herself regarding the verdict, I just had to pose a relevant question to her–even though I knew the answer would be, "No."

I simply asked her, "Are you, in some way, related to Nicole Simpson or Ron Goldman? Or did you personally know either one of them?"

Of course, the woman didn't bother to address my query and blew me off for being absurd and ridiculous. But I wasn't finished having my say. "You're so pissed off," I added, "a person would think O.J. killed your momma. One little black man slips through the judicial cracks, and you're about to blow a darn gasket. Where was your outrage when all the innocent black men were convicted and punished for crimes they didn't even commit? When they were unjustly lynched and incarcerated? Where the hell were you then, huh?"

It goes without saying, I wasn't regarded as a favourite person by the teacher I verbally lambasted that day, but I learned to live with her disdain. I have always despised hypocrisy and selective righteousness–and especially when it's solely based on skin colour.

However, when I consider the sexual woes of a black man named "Clarence Thomas," conservative Caucasian men (and some white women too) showed me that they have a different side to them. Down deep, they were still contemptuous of a person's skin colour but as long as that dark person "carries their water for them" (meaning, the select person is aligned with their racist agenda), they are able to squeeze their noses and throw their political support behind him. Therefore, since Thomas fitted that description to a tee, his voyage to the Supreme Court was subjected to smooth waters.

Certainly, that was why those conservative white men in Congress elected to denigrate Anita Hill, who accused Thomas of sexual impropriety, and, essentially, throw her under the bus. In their self-interest, those men cared less than a flying damn about the merit of Miss Hill's complaint. And that's a prime example of political hypocrisy.

Sorrowfully though, white men have not cornered the market on that concept either. When that "Access Hollywood" tape came out and white women were keenly made aware of the true character of Donald Trump, they were not remotely turned off or repulsed by his behavior.

Evidently, those white women could barely wait to get to the polls and cast their ballots for him. And that says something about those women, not Trump. Who knows? Maybe, they are wedded to men who act like Trump. Perhaps, after being thrilled and flattered that their individual spouses could hardly keep his hands off of them in the past, they eventually realized that their husbands are hard-pressed to keep his hands off of any woman. And maybe, also, their own spouses, similar to men like the Donald, ascribe to the barbarian philosophy, 'If you can't be with the one you usually grope; then grope the one you're with.' Who really knows?

It is my greatest hope that the "Me-Too" movement goes forward without racism, hypocrisy and double standards.

Being an intricate part of it, this country is notoriously flagrant

Racism, Sexism, Trumpism, Pseudo-Christianity and the Cinema

with double standards. Undoubtedly, if Barack Obama had acted like Donald Trump when he was the President of the United States, he would be facing impeachment. Imagine Mr. Obama's voice on that infamous tape. If the opioid problem was solely existent in the black community, it would not be considered a "crisis." And Jeff Sessions would have called for an upsurge in criminalization. If the average school shooter was black, instead of white, the National Rifles Association (the N.R.A.) would push back on the production of assault weaponry. And, again, Attorney General Sessions would have called for an upsurge in criminalization.

Prayerfully, the "Me-Too" movement has staying power.

It's not enough to weed out and dethrone sexual predators in the communications and media industry. Men, mostly white ones, have ran this country for centuries. They have had a stranglehold on it. And most of those men are archaic, entrenched in their power and firmly set in their ways.

Here, in 2018, it is time for marked change, innovation and new blood. Therefore, with women coming into their own, standing up for their rights and gaining real prominence, it may produce a better country and a better world also. And the female persuasion might emerge successful–if they avoid the mistakes made by their male counter parts. Who knows?

Perhaps, they'll even hammer a stake into the hearts of blatant hypocrisy, double standards and rampant racism as well. And upon doing so, then maybe, just maybe, America might achieve the long-aspired but very-elusive "greatness" it continually craves, a stellar eminence that's embraced by the entire nation, and not just the privileged horde.

However, since the "Me-Too" movement is relatively new (in its embryonic stage), I would be remiss in not making a few provocative and hard-line observations. I don't mean to sound the "spoiler alert," but I feel compelled to make them. Again, I am trying to keep it real.

Firstly, in the Spring of 2018, the American public learned that long-time comedian and mega-television personality, Bill Cosby, was finally found guilty of sexual misconduct and perversion that allegedly occurred decades ago. And, at present, Mr. Cosby is facing substantial prison time and, I'm sure, a vast monetary penance too. I emphasized, both, "finally" and "allegedly" because the accused "black man" (Cosby) was subjected to a retrial and, in spite of the absence of concrete or even trace evidence, despite eyewitness testimony (except from the mouths of the subject victims), the elderly comedian was "brought to justice."

Personally, I don't know if Bill Cosby was guilty as charged (certainly, I was not on hand to observe his scandalous conduct), but I do know this:

Over the years, there have been numerous women who accused Cosby of sexual impropriety and seduction, and most of those assaults affiliated with drugs. Of course, I can't discredit those claims either. But unless the renowned TV icon's victims were from the planet Venus, they knew the man was married to Camille Cosby in real life and to Claire Huxtable in sit-com life. You may very well brand me judgmental or somewhat prudish, but why did any of those reported victims go to Cosby's respective hotel rooms?

I would wager fifty dollars against a cake donut that the majority of them had heard of the notorious "casting couch," made infamous in the 1930's, 1940's, 1950's and beyond. And even if they were not knowledgeable of that seductive mechanism, in their apparent naiveté, did they actually think Bill Cosby was interested in playing tiddlywinks or a game of scrabble when they stepped over his room's threshold? I mean, what's up with that? I only hope that the many female supporters of the "Me-Too" movement are not advocating the, "Women, good and Men, bad" mentality. That sounds much too much like the double-standard premise to me.

Secondly, when I occasionally reflect back to my woman associate who took it upon herself to seek out her husband's outside girlfriend and scold her to a fare-thee–well, I always emerge

Racism, Sexism, Trumpism, Pseudo-Christianity and the Cinema

awestruck in the wake of the wife's gall and tenacity. I am quite familiar with the adage, "All is fair in love and war," but, to me, it's a crock of unadulterated bull crap. It's a saying that is called to mind by classic wrongdoers—in an attempt to justify her or his unsavory conduct. And I believe it's akin to another adage, "The end justifies the means,"which I intend to take issue with later on in this written text.

Personally speaking, I was married for a period of 28 years (from 1979 until 2007) and if my wife had survived breast cancer, I am relatively sure we would still be together today. Admittedly though, I have never stood witness to a perfect marriage, and I would be lying if I claimed mine was.

But, owing to a dallying and errant father, I never cheated on my wife. And I honestly believe, neither did she disperse her romantic affection elsewhere during our 28 years. Seemingly, my spouse was restrained by religious conviction and I, on the other hand, was virtually obsessed with not being like my dad. (Sometimes, a person can transform a negative into a positive). Frankly, I loved my father but I was never partial to his amorous ways.

I said all of the foregoing to, eventually, state the following: Marriage is oftentimes a tough and frustrating lifestyle. Like most one-on-one relationships it is froth with frequent "ups and down" and "highs and lows." And unless the wedded couple ascribes to the wise words in an old time Petula Clark song, their relationship (and despite the sexual component) will be a daunting and uphill climb.

Miss Clark's yesteryear song was entitled "Don't Sleep on the Subway" and the specific lyric I'm referring to is, 'You must realize that it's all compromise' and plainly stated it means that each party must be resigned to "give" and to "take." In most cases, no one is all right and no one is all wrong either. "You give me my just-do and I, in return, will give you yours."

But, sometimes, even when things appear to be flowing smoothly surface-wise in a marital union, a sudden and unexpected storm pops up. One-half of the betrothed couple (usually, the man), peering through a roving and lustful eye, comes to believe that "the grass is greener on the other side." He meets that other woman (at a bar, his work-site, or somewhere), apprises her of all the failings and faults of his "homebody" spouse, and the very attentive and sympathetic listener takes it all into account—and the resultant affair begins to take shape.

I know it all sounds so simplistic and rather juvenile too and, sometimes, it's just that. For instance—a lady admirer of mine once told me, "If you weren't married, you'd be my kind of man." Now, maybe, the average man would have been flattered and all puffed up, but I'm discerning and, again, I try and keep it real too. Therefore, I smilingly responded, "But I happen to know you're in a long-time relationship with a married man, so what are you really saying to me?"

Of course, I can be entirely in error or purely mistaken, and I have no substantial proof of it either, but I have always believed that women are smarter than men. (I imagine it's because women think with the head attached to their necks). But, over the years (and I'm fully aware I'll face chiding, criticism and strong lambasting over this) I've come to believe, too, that women, in general, don't particularly like other women. If that was not true, then there would not be so many complicit "mistresses" waiting in the wings to accommodate unfaithful husbands.

If those applicable women cared a single iota about fellow women; their long-suffering, their anguish and their mental well-being, they would entertain some degree of reluctance or moral turpitude.

Instead, it's "full speed ahead" for many of them.

It's "hooray for me and the hell with the man's wife" (and that, by the way, means the hell with the man's children also).

Those women can slice and dice it any way they wish, they can concoct any lame-brain rationalization they can, but they are

Racism, Sexism, Trumpism, Pseudo-Christianity and the Cinema

basically and acutely aware of the damage they cause–and, despite their smartness, they plainly do not care!

Believe it or not, I'm not trying to be the moral cop here. Grown people do what they're big enough to do. But I do have a series of questions to pose here. Hearkening back to my "mad hatter" associate, the woman who elected to have it out with her husband's girlfriend, I'd like to know:

1. Why, after being the "other woman" when the subject man was married to his first wife, did she think he would be faithful to her?
2. Since she was formerly playing the outside woman role, how could she be upset and so incensed with her replacement?
3. Why did she, and any dallying woman (after inflicting a ton of grief on her married lover's spouse and children), think it would be smooth-sailing ahead for her?

In fairy-tale land, why did she think she would be "happily ever after?" And, in Christendom land, why should she be in God's good graces or favor? Although it's not very nice, sometimes I feel urged to ask, "Who the hell do you think you are?"

While numerous readers might regard me as somewhat crass and, maybe, coarsely judgmental at this precise juncture as well, I would truly like to hear the answers to the questions I posed above. It would be therapeutic for me. I have dwelled on similar queries throughout my lengthy life. Perhaps, just perhaps, the budding "Me-Too" movement will include them in their ongoing focus and agenda. I certainly hope so.

Trumpism

"All staunch Donald Trump supporters are not racist, but all racist are staunch Donald Trump supporters!"

The Art of Making America Hate Again

In 2016 and 2017, when Donald J. Trump was running for President of the United States, I was continually aggravated by his standard campaign slogan and the various news reporters who frequently dialogued with the Republican candidate as well. Being an elderly black man, a fellow who has been on the scene for quite a while, I have always been totally in the dark (pun intended) regarding the phrase "Make America Great Again." Admittedly, this country has done a lot of commendable and even benevolent things, but "greatness" is rather elusive and vague. Similar to "beauty," it is in the eye of the beholder.

As I stated, I was dually irritated by the assorted reporters who were on hand during the campaign also. Part of their jobs, in my estimation, was to ask the tough questions. And unless they were apprised of the answers and elected to keep them to his or herself, I felt it was most appropriate to ask Mr. Trump, "In your personal opinion, when was America great and when did it lose its greatness?" Enquiring minds (such as mine) would like to know!

Had I been a newsman, I am certain I would have been branded brash and overbearing. Because I would have asked The Donald' a series of queries. Such as: Was America great prior to Barack Obama's presidency? Or, maybe, during the George W.

Racism, Sexism, Trumpism, Pseudo-Christianity and the Cinema

Bush administration? Was it at its greatest in the 50's, the 60's, the 70's–when? Or–was it great during a yesteryear era when blacks and other minorities "knew their lowly place" and when white folks brutally and essentially "ran the damn place?"

It is commonly said in the judicial field that an attorney should not ask a question (especially during a trial) that he, the attorney, does not already know the authentic answer to. Therefore, when I reflect back to the reporters who had the opportunity to converse with then-candidate Trump (and especially the white ones), I believe, possibly, they were privy to the definitive answers. I only wish they would have shared those answers with me and the American public. It would have been positively revealing.

Call me slow-witted or plain-old nosey, but I was in a state of confusion throughout the duration of the Trump campaign. There were a lot of rally-cries that rose out of that campaign that, both, perplexed and tickled me. For example, one day when I was in my home's kitchen, and within earshot of my TV set in the living room, I heard an irate male voice shout,

"We're gonna take back our country!"

Right away, I dropped what I was doing in my kitchen and proceeded to the living room, fully expecting to observe the fired-up "Native American" who voiced that remark. But to my surprise, it was a red-faced white man! At that point, I became angry myself and, simultaneously, a number of relevant queries popped into my mind. For a moment, I imagined I was addressing the infuriated man on my television screen. As if he was actually within hearing range of me, I asked, "Are you so dumb and ignorant that you're not aware that your ancestors murdered and nearly wiped out a whole race of people who were native to America? All in a fierce effort to annex and confiscate a habitant that was already populated? And, incidentally, they did the same thing to Mexican people when it came to Texas."

Then momentarily, owing to that very after-thought, I found myself hearkening back to a movie I once saw. That film, a western, was entitled "Valdez is Coming" and it had Burt Lancaster portraying a Mexican peace officer. Earlier, in the movie, it was disclosed that Valdez (Lancaster) had formerly served as a tracker of Apache Indians for the U.S. cavalry. But later, when someone asked Valdez, "How long did you track the Apache?", he replied,

"Until I know'd better." In essence, he was saying, 'Until I came to realize that Mexicans were hated just as much as Indians were, and especially by the white man. At least, that's what I read between the lines.

But back to the disgruntled Caucasian man who was on my TV screen. Once again, I was critical of the on-site news media. Even if I was just a cub-reporter, I would have posed a few valid questions to the man. If I yielded to the claim that people who looked like him authentically "owned" America, I would have asked him, "Who, in fact, has your country and how and when did they take possession of it?

To be completely honest, I know I'm seeking answers to queries that cannot legitimately be addressed. Well-entrenched falsehoods and hypocrisy ride roughshod with the answers. But, still, when I reflect on the "Trump phenomenon" (and that's how I see it), yet another very troubling and serious question comes to mind.

However, I'm not mindless of an answer to it, for I'm already privy to the answer. The ruminating query is actually derived from a yesteryear radio production, a "then" popular serial drama which was entitled "The Shadow," and it came on the air, vocally quizzing, "Who knows what evil lurks in the hearts of man?" By design, the forthright answer was "the shadow knows."

Although The Shadow was a fictional character, real-life history shows us that evil not only exists, it stands ready to assist and aid every zealot and madman who craves and covets power. It drove Italy's Benito Mussolini and Germany's Adolf Hitler, it inspired America's Senator Joseph McCarthy and Reverend Jim Jones and, most certainly, it explains Donald Trump's mercurial and maniacal appeal. He is an individual who not only feeds

Racism, Sexism, Trumpism, Pseudo-Christianity and the Cinema

and salivates on the fears and bigotries of hateful, self-absorbed Caucasians, he gladly welcomes it. Show me a person who faults others for their own life failures and roadblocks, and I'll show you a Donald Trump supporter and loyalist.

Am I suggesting that the American president is evil-incarnated? No, I am not. Am I hinting that Trump is the prophetic "antichrist?" I say "no" to that particular query too. (I don't believe the man is affiliated with any faith). Furthermore, am I calling the President's base collectively abominable and totally mean-spirited? No, not really. I am saying something quite simple actually. Something that people generally dismiss and gloss over.

There is nothing disparaging or derogatory I can say about Donald J. Trump that hasn't already been said numerous times during the past two years or so, but I'm focusing on something about the man that should be important to every conscientious and well-meaning parent in America. It is undisputable and verifiable, too, that our Commander-in-Chief is not a nice or decent person. And if you see him in a different light, then it says something markedly revealing about you. Either you're cut from the same cloth (like a Jeff Sessions and a John Kelly), or you're self-centered and void of empathy.

I purposely singled out parents above because I fully realize that there's a large segment of Trump supporters who would vehemently scoff at my criticism of the sitting President. He could actually be Beelzebub in the flesh and they would still defend him to the very hilt. He even once bragged he could shoot someone down in the street and nothing would happen to him and, in theory, he was right. Even in the midst of denouncing my assessment of him, the majority of his followers could care less about Trump's unscrupulous persona.

It's not because they are collectively stupid or naive, however, it's because they have found comfort in their disingenuousness. Instead of dwelling on the President's substandard character, I am sure they would swiftly change the subject. Similar to the puppet members of the Republican party, they would choose to talk about tax breaks, the stock market and the Bully-in-Chief's isolationist agenda, any and every topic except the main one: The man's character.

But my target audience is America's parents and many of them may very well be amongst the foregoing group but they best think long and hard about my original assessment.

Donald Trump is not a nice person and I never heard that said about any preceding Commander-in-Chief in my long lifetime.

Sure, some individuals might retreat to that old adage, "Nice guys finish last" but even if there's a degree of truism in it, at least they finish and they are constantly rooted on by similar-minded people, people who are decent, loving and supportive. I don't know about you (the reader) as a parent, but I have always prayed that my three kids would be highly regarded and esteemed as they travel along life's road. In fact, I wish that for your children also.

Personally, I have tried my best to be an inspiration and a role model for my two sons and daughter. I have constantly tried to practice what I preach and live a righteous life. I'm not perfect, no one is, but I have consistently encouraged my kids to form relationships with wholesome and upstanding people. I remind them, too, that while they can't handpick their relatives, they do have the luxury to select their close-knit friends and associates.

As I alluded to before, sometimes a person can reference a blatant negative and arrive at an ultimate positive.

And that brings me back to Donald J. Trump. Thanks to God's grace, my children are all adults at present. However, if they were still young and impressionable, I would explicitly tell them not to be remotely like the current POTUS and try to avoid being in the presence of anyone who shares his personality traits.

Incidentally, I would not have issued similar advice to my children regarding Barack Obama or George W. Bush either. But

Racism, Sexism, Trumpism, Pseudo-Christianity and the Cinema

neither of those presidents stooped to mock a physically-challenged American citizen and nor did they call black NFL football players "sons-of-bitches."

In addition, those two former Chief Executives did not galvanize their rowdy base to call for the jailing of a female political opponent (Hillary Clinton—"Lock her up! "), neither of them denigrated a military war hero (John McCain), they didn't resort to juvenile name-calling and mean-spirited verbal put-downs and neither of them boasted about grabbing women by their private parts either.

All of the foregoing, I find despicable and shameful. Still, Trump's base remains intact. Some people used to call Ronald Reagan the "Teflon President" but Donald Trump epitomizes that term. And it's not that the man can't do anything wrong, it's solely because wrongdoing is irrelevant and immaterial to his supporters. Donald Trump could be a cross between Theodore "Ted" Bundy and Jeffrey Dahmer and they would still rally behind him.

As long as the President promotes their personal agendas and biasness, they don't mind him being a scum-bag and a international embarrassment. So what if the man is a chronic liar, a sexual predator, a womanizer, an egotistical braggart or a closet racist? None of that seems to matter, and especially to individuals who subscribe to the mind-set that 'the end justifies the means.'

However, when those self-absorbed people emerge from their cocoons, what about their bystanding loved ones who once respected and esteemed them? What about innocent children who, at times, looked towards them for moral support and guidance? Furthermore, what about something called integrity and righteousness? Can those steadfast Trump followers honestly say, if circumstances presented itself, that they would be overjoyed to have a father (or mother), a son (or daughter), a husband (or wife) or even a dear friend like the present POTUS? And if they come forth with an affirmative reply to that hypothetical query, then I suggest that they seriously rethink it, that is without being fixated on "the Donald's" reported wealth. Either way, I offer my sincere condolences to them.

However, consider the following too: If you are an individual who finds solace in "the end justifies the means," I suggest that you read the heartbreaking saga of the Joseph P. Kennedy family. They were billionaires too, like Trump, and the patriarch amassed a fortune by any means necessary. It is well-known that tragedy played an intricate part in the Kennedy's lives. And remember this, too, it is said that the sins of the father are, sometimes, revisited on the sons.

Then again, if you are disinterested or unmoved by the true story of the Kennedy clan, maybe you'll focus on the fictionalized account of the Don Vito Corleone family. In the 'Godfather Parts 1 and 2' they occasionally talked about be coming "legitimate" (supplanting all of their past ruthless and criminal deeds) and becoming prominent and successful in the not-too-distant future. However, in the 'Godfather Part 3' Don Michael Corleone was made to suffer the ultimate comeuppance. His beloved and adored daughter, Mary, was shot to death, inadvertently taking a bullet that was really meant for him. Eventually, Don Michael Corleone died a lonely and broken man.

Certainly, one can dismiss the cinema account alluded to above and the awful tragedies that befell the real-life Kennedy family too (People are good at rationalizing, saying that will not happen to me), but we reap what we sow and repercussions are not always only resigned to hell. Ever so often, people are subjected to hell on earth.

I recently heard the current POTUS, of all people, tell the 'snake story.' You know the one about the old lady who found a wounded, poisonous snake? She took the reptile home, nursed it back to health and ended up getting bitten by it. Then, as the old woman was dying, the snake boldly declared, "Well, you knew I was a snake–before you went and took me in."

Sitting in front of my TV and hearing that story, I soon asked

Racism, Sexism, Trumpism, Pseudo-Christianity and the Cinema

myself, "Doesn't Trump's base realize that their idol fits the snake's profile? Well, when I reflect on the President's followers who are now souring on him (and there are quite a few), if they are even slightly honest with themselves, then they have to admit that they helped elect the exact "snake" they so dearly cherished. With all of his idiosyncrasies and abrasive flaws, Trump has always been Trump.

To my utter dismay, the least concern of disenchanted Donald Trump voters revolves around the race issue. The man has always been a classic racist and when he remarked (and I'm paraphrasing here) "I'm the least racist person you have ever met," he became a comical, classic racist. When I first heard him voice that bizarre statement, I told myself that he makes Governor George Wallace look like St. Francis of Assisi. I just wonder if the man believes that if you keep making the same declaration over and over again, no matter how disingenuous you are, then people will come to buy into it.

It is commonly said that, "The apple doesn't fall far from the tree" and since the President's father was notoriously discriminatory to Negroes in the housing arena, his privileged son essentially followed in his old man's footsteps. But "the Donald" took it up a notch. From his outrageous behavior in the days of the so-called 'Central Park Five' to his contemporary disparaging of black National League football players, he has shown his racist skirt. Let's face it, the POTUS suffers from 'Obama-encephalitis (Obama-on-the-brain). He intensely hates the former black president and is hell-bent on destroying and dismantling every accomplishment the former administration made, not only the repeal of the Affordable Care Act. Even after being proven wrong regarding the infamous 'birther issue,' Trump is obsessed with verbally denigrating his black predecessor. And what that's all about, I believe only a qualified psychiatrist could determine.

Unfortunately, though, no matter how much I or others criticize Trump, he and his administration has already caused immeasurable harm to the black community. And it's a "harm" that has tremendous staying power. Just by being elected the POTUS, he was endowed with the power to appoint Federal judges. And since his selection list is comprised of "conservative" candidates and the subsequent appointments are for life, Afro-American citizens who have future run-ins with the law apparatus will be in the greatest of peril.

Now, I could be wrong or even paranoid, but I've always regarded the term 'conservative' as a code word for seasoned racial bigots. I not only believe that individuals of that ilk are bent on keeping the system status quo, they'd love to return to the way things were in the 1940's and priorly. Not to be facetious, but was that when America was great?

Not long ago, I shared my foretasted argument with a dear friend of mine. I asked him, "What do you think now?"

And that was because he had once mouthed something that Trump questioned when he was still on the campaign trail. In an attempt to garner presidential votes for himself, Trump singled out black citizens and quizzed, "What do you have to lose?"

President Trump is a clever and crafty man; I've got to give that to him. If he played a musical instrument like he plays biased Caucasian people, he would be a renown virtuoso. That's exactly what he did when the black NFL athletes were 'taking a knee' in protest of police brutality. Instead of considering it for what it really was, he elected to muddy the waters by tossing the American flag into the mix. The protest had nothing to do with patriotism, or the flag, but he knew he was pulling the racist strings of his base. If he wasn't attune to anything else about America, he realizes how deep and pervasive the racial divide is.

Evidently though, Donald Trump's racist temperament spans way beyond America's borders. In mid-January of this year (2018) the President audaciously referred to Haiti and African nations as "shit-hole" countries and then turned right around and vocalized his personal preference for welcoming white immigrants from

Racism, Sexism, Trumpism, Pseudo-Christianity and the Cinema

Norway to our country. Certainly, I am not a mind-reader or a soothsayer, but I firmly believe he dared to make those prejudicial comments because he felt ultra-comfortable in his skin and his select setting. He was meeting with cabinet members who were all white and he felt they were totally in sync with his mind-set.

And Trump was right on point too. The majority of the individuals in that subject meeting seemed to not only share his ideology, they were just as skilled in lying and stonewalling as he is also. While some of his cohorts later claimed the President had not made the insulting remarks at all, others insisted that they had not heard it. Then, when it was determined that Trump did, indeed, make those ugly comments, they were casually brushed off as a mere "joke." Several other times when the POTUS was decried by the American public, the administration's shameless mouthpieces tried to frame them as jokes also.

Each time, when they retreated to that shabby, superficial excuse (jokes), I found myself thinking of a movie I once saw. It was entitled 'Ragtime' and it starred the late actors Howard Rollins and James Cagney. It took place in the early 1900's (around the turn of the century) and it focused on a newly-purchased automobile, probably a T-model Ford. On the surface, buying a new car doesn't sound like much of a plot or subplot but since the automobile was costly and its owner was a "colored" man (Rollins), it puts forth an interesting scenario.

Since I saw it, I'll divulge what it was. Solely because Rollins was a black man and he was driving a brand new motor vehicle around town, a group of resentful and jealous-hearted white men decided it was an affront to their racial superiority. Therefore, they confiscated the automobile and took turns "defecating" inside of it.

The plot thickened when an infuriated Howard

Rollins and several of his close-knit cohorts forcefully took over an artifacts-filled museum and refused to peacefully come out. The black occupiers were fully aware that the materials in their immediate midst were considered priceless and virtually irreplaceable and, therefore, were not overly fearful of a violent reprisal from the on-scene police presence.

Then, came the city's Chief of Police (Jimmy Cagney's final big screen appearance) and when he was apprised of what prompted the hostile museum take-over, he instantly demanded that the head honcho involved in the nasty, unsavory offense, who happened to be the city's fire chief, come to the scene. Not only that, but Cagney strenuously told the fire chief to proceed to the adjacent museum and apologize to Rollins.

Naturally, the fire chief strongly balked at the idea. (After all, Rollins was a "colored" man). The chief was so resistant, in fact, he decried, "What's wrong with that nigger? Can't he take a joke?"

Sadly, and regretfully, 'Ragtime' was based on a true story. Therefore, in the aftermath of that insincere apology and when Rollins finally dropped his arms and peacefully emerged from the museum, he was promptly shot dead. That was par for the course.

Shortly after Donald Trump's 2018 State of the Union Address, he accused members of the Black Caucus of treason.

Why? Because that select group did not collectively applaud him when he bragged about decreasing black unemployment during the address. Spoiler alert! Since job discrimination is no longer legal or lawful in America, when there's an upsurge in white employment, black employment subsequently increases a notch also.

Therefore, the President was undeserving of a rousing handclap or ovation. Notably though, when Trump was strongly criticized for his insulting "treason" comment, it, too, was spinned as a mere joke.

On a personal note, I am a person who actually loves to laugh. In addition, I like to tell jokes and I am known for regularly sharing them with other people. My sense of humor is a part of my personality and always has been. Therefore, when I hear someone tell a joke or make a witty remark, I automatically chuckle. I can't speak for other people, but I don't need the Trump machine to tell me what's funny or mildly amusing. But I must add, if Trump and his lockstep spokespersons extract any humor whatsoever from hearing NFL players called "sons-of-bitches," elected congressmen labeled "treasonous," struggling, poor nations branded "shit-hole countries" and a distinguished terminally-ill senator being told "he's dying any way," they direly need to hire another joke writer. Because none of the foregoing is remotely funny or clever. In fact, they're somewhat sick, mean-spirited and hateful. And in some ways they rank right up there with the so-called joke — when those crude white men took a dump in the black man's newly-bought car.

Birds of a Feather Flock Together

In the past, I was never an individual who painted either political party with a broad brush (not the Democrats or the Republicans). I truly believed there were decent and upstanding public servants in both parties. However, owing to the "Trump phenomenon," I am sad to admit that I have gradually undergone a mental metamorphosis.

Call me idealistic or even naive if you wish, but I used to think that when men and women ran for congress they were genuinely concerned with the well-being of our nation.

I realized that some of them had hidden agendas but I was gullible enough to displace those agendas as secondary and matter-of-factly.

But when Donald Trump became America's Chief Executive and began behaving like an egocentric dictator instead of a stable-minded president, I took an in-depth look at his Republican cohorts and began to question where their collective and individual heads were.

Would they concern themselves with the welfare of our country or the ever-changing, rather bizarre whims of President Donald J. Trump? Thus far, the latter concern is winning out.

There is nothing new under the sun regarding Trump, not to me or any clear-thinking person. Ever since the man practically lost his mind, calling for the conviction of the "Central Park 5" (who were, alternately, found innocent) and then obsessed over the "birther" conspiracy about Barack Obama, I have been acutely aware of who he really is. The only good thing to be extracted from his 2016 election is the underlying message he sends to non-voters, especially the ones of African heritage. Over the years I heard far too many fellow black men say, "My vote doesn't count" or "It doesn't matter who the President is" and I pray that the Trump phenomenon is a wakeup call for them. I'm sincerely hoping it will send them to the polls in the near future.

With that said, I'd like to focus on the bedrock of the Trump presidency; his fellow Republicans in the Congress. Admittedly, I am a Democrat but that does not mean that I've always been totally anti-Republican. Until Donald Trump came into power, I had certain respect for a number of Republican politicians, and not only the ones who actively opposed him on the campaign trail. But at present, it is alarmingly apparent that unless a Republican senator or representative is scheduled to leave the political scene (not run again), the fixed Republicans have no qualms or shame in climbing aboard a Trump steamship.

Many of them not only toss principles and integrity to the wind, they're not above taking to the air ways (television and radio) in an effort to sanitize their President's rather putrid insanity. For instance, I never liked Orrin Hatch but even in my distaste for the GOP senator, I prolongly considered him to be sincere and resolute. But when he came out this year (2016) and declared that Trump was one of The "great" presidents in history, I keenly realized the terrible devastation caused by dementia. Hatch is slated to retire

Racism, Sexism, Trumpism, Pseudo-Christianity and the Cinema

and leave the Congress. Upon making asinine claims like that, the man should have been on the "bon voyage" plane "yesterday!

I will hand this to America's current POTUS. Although his hiring mechanics are out of whack and unorthodox too (he has dismissed so many people in his administration thus far that he should consider having a revolving door installed at the White House), he is hell-bent on surrounding himself with like-minded individuals, people who are in total lockstep with his agenda and erratic personality (also, known as "yes men").

Evidently, even though Trump is wishy-washy and impulsive as well, he's steadily doing just that. In my personal viewpoint, however, I believe he "drained the swamp" he always alluded to, he retained all the creatures that once lurked there and gradually incorporated them into his bizarre administration.

I persistently shake my head and laugh when I hear speculation about Donald Trump firing Attorney General Jeff Sessions. I find it absurd because the President and Sessions are practically two peas in a pod. They think alike and share similar ideoligies, especially when it comes to Afro-Americans and immigrants. With Sessions in his vantage position, Trump is poised to undo every legislative stride that was made by the foregoing Barack Obama administration. And that's imperative to the President. Therefore, the POTUS would be hard pressed to give the AG his walking papers.

The current Chief of Staff, Gen. John Kelly, is an ideal fit for Donald Trump also. In a sense, they are brothers in-arms. Seemingly, the two have similar temperaments, matching dispassionate natures and (although Trump never served a single day in the armed forces) have stern military minds.

And that assessment was acutely evident when it came to the black soldier who lost his life in Africa in 2017.

When Sgt. LaDavid Johnson was killed in Niger, I honestly believe the President was at a loss for words. He did not know what his response should be. Therefore, since he was well aware that his Chief of Staff's son had died in military action, Trump sought a degree of insight from Kelly. I can't rightfully criticize him for doing that, it was a rational thought, but if the President had any authentic empathy inside of him at all, he would have deleted part of the advice that Kelly shared with him.

Upon talking about the grievous fate of his own son, the general indicated that one of his friends (in the wake of the tragedy) reminded him that his son had "signed up for it," meaning his boy had volunteered for the military. Now, I was in the army for three years, I even escorted a deceased soldier's body to his hometown (admittedly, I never was a general), but I can't imagine finding any solace from being told that my fallen loved one had "signed up for it. In fact, I would find it difficult to identify the spokesman as a friend. But, still, when the Commander-in-Chief gave his condolences to Sergeant Johnson's distraught widow via telephone, he mouthed that rather insensitive phrase also.

Maybe I'm guilty of nit-picking or, maybe, I'm being ultra-sensitive myself, but would you (the reader) want someone to add such a footnote to a condolence extended to you?

Additionally, if you were a police officer's spouse and your husband or wife was killed in the line of duty, would you find any comfort whatsoever in having someone say, "He (or she) signed up for it?"

I enlisted in the service way back in the 1960's, but it never crossed my mind that I was going to die for my country. It was possible (especially, with the Vietnam War looming) but it was never my game-plan. Another general, a renown one named George S. Patton, once declared that in war time, "Soldiers should not be so willing to die for their country, but should, instead, try and make the opposing S.O.B. die for his country." Anyhow, that was the main thrust of Patton's World War II avocation and it is certainly food for thought. Regardless though, since the President was unable to summon sincere and heartfelt sympathy or empathy

Racism, Sexism, Trumpism, Pseudo-Christianity and the Cinema

on his own during the La David Johnson episode, I will say it one more time. Donald J. Trump is not a nice person!

Sex, Lies and Hypocrisy

It is almost impossible to talk about Donald Trump without bringing up Hillary Clinton. Not because they're joined at the hip or even because Clinton was Trump's Democratic opponent during the 2016 presidential election. In my personal estimation, the campaign itself revealed something very profound and telling about the American electorate, especially when it came to Caucasian women.

When the "Access Holly wood" tape was released to the public (the tape that captured Trump boasting about crudely molesting women), a great deal of people thought it would be a game-changer. Many of them thought that that tape would essentially doom Donald Trump's chance at becoming president of the United States. Focusing on America's white women, it was widely assumed that that group would be so appalled and outraged in the wake of that tape that they would turn against Trump in droves. That thought-pattern was plainly wrong.

I wasn't surprised in the least. Not because I'm so brilliant or insightful, but because my memory is long and quite vivid. When I think back to women like Monica Lewinski and Paula Jones, I recall that backlash that was visited on the First Lady by white women at that time. Although they were furious regarding President Bill Clinton's infidelity and dallying, they seemed especially angry with Hillary.

When that story was grabbing the headlines, I was working with four Caucasian female teachers and three of them were vocally upset with Mrs. Clinton. One of those women even criticized Hillary for not, alternately, divorcing the, then, POTUS. I recall her stating, "If Bill Clinton was my husband, I'd leave him so fast it would make his damn head swim.

I didn't issue a reply, but I really wanted to. I felt like telling her, "No, you would probably divorce Hillary's husband—all because you don't love Hillary's husband and nor do you share a child with him."

If infidelity and unfaithfulness was the supreme motive behind divorce in this country, fatherless homes would spiral to epidemic proportions.

If the average American wife refused to 'stand by her man' (like Hillary Clinton did), there would be more broken marriages than broken commandments.

I had an interesting confrontation with my own, beloved mother one afternoon. Mom was giving advice to a young married woman at the time, a woman who was tearful because her husband was 'playing around' with several outside women. My mother was 'old school' and she sincerely meant well with her counsel, but when she told the distraught young lady, "As long as he brings his money home on payday, try and weather the storm. Men are gonna always mess around," I was livid!

"Momma, please don't tell her that," I inserted.

"If she was screwin' around on him, he couldn't take it! Suppose he infects her with a sexual disease? Plus, what kind of example is he setting for his boys, huh? She should confront his dog-ass behind!"

Of course, my mother didn't appreciate me throwing in my two-cents. She even told me to mind my own business and, jokingly, told me to "go to my room." However, as I mentioned, my mom was old-school, meaning she was from an era when men equated their manhood with sexual conquest and tomfoolery.

In the same vein, that's why Caucasian women (and a segment of females in other races also) were not notably upset or outraged by the Access Hollywood tape that outted Donald Trump. As I suggested a while back, I'm not adamant about it but I surmise

Racism, Sexism, Trumpism, Pseudo-Christianity and the Cinema

that many of their respective husbands, from time to time, behaved similarly. Only the wives, themselves, knew the truth.

But back to the "Hillary Clinton haters." And that's what I call those white women who practically lost their minds, begrudging the First Lady in the 1990's and at present also.

In the midst of the campaign, I asked myself, "What exactly fuels their insidious loathing?"

I further reasoned that Hillary Clinton had been a social advocate and a public servant for almost forty (40) years and the 'E-mail' controversy was relatively new. So, it had to be something else! Who really knows? Maybe, she poisoned the family dog or kidnapped the family cat. (I am being somewhat facetious now). When people used to say, "I just don't trust her," I would ask them, "Why? Do you know her personally?"To me, it's like a white person scoping me out and stating, "There's something about you that I really don't like. I just can't put my finger on it." And, of course, I'd simply counter with, "If you did put your finger on it, I can assure you it will not rub off."

When I look even further back at Hillary Clinton when she was the First Lady, I recall when she was trying to implement universal health care. She didn't succeed, but she did try. However, that essentially has been a desire sponsored by the Democratic party. Seemingly, the Republicans were never sincere or adamant in bringing forth a comprehensive health plan but, apparently, they love being obstructionist when one comes into existence (such as the Affordable Care Act).

Upon returning to the Hillary Clinton saga and her haters and distracters, and especially white women, we must remember that they loathed President Bill Clinton also (or even more). In the 1990's and during Clinton's presidency, that specified group claimed it was because of his extramarital affairs (as if they exuded even an inkling of sympathy for the First Lady) and loudly called for his, subsequent, impeachment.

Where, then, are those boisterous, self-righteous critics at present? Even if their moral compasses were, somehow, damaged or broken over the years, why haven't they taken out time to have them repaired? In the wake of the current POTUS cavorting with prostitutes and established porn stars, where is their outrage? Plus, why aren't they berating Melania Trump for tolerating his despicable and scandalous behavior? It smells like unadulterated hypocrisy to me, and a chronic case of selective righteousness as well.

During the campaign, when Donald Trump had the audacity to parade out a group of women who accused Bill Clinton of sexual improprieties, Trump's base sneered and applauded them. What was that all about? Bill Clinton wasn't running for a third term! That bizarre maneuver only made sense to crude and vindictive-minded individuals.

And, by the way, the current POTUS needs to publicly apologize to his long-suffering spouse, Melania. Why? Because as she goes through the motions of denouncing and decrying "bullying," he makes her look hypocritical also. It has to be exasperating and disheartening to know you're wedded to the supreme Bully-in-Chief!

To be honest, I feel sorry for Melania, and my heart goes out to the Donald's son, Baron, also. All the money in the world cannot render a person happy. You, as a reader of this piece, may very well consider me to be the "perennial nobody" I alluded to earlier, but I do know that much. It's a mite too late to save Trump's older children (they have been exposed to their dad much too long), but it's not too late for young Baron. As I suggested priorly, sometimes you can extract a "positive" from a "negative." And it would behoove Melania, as a loving and nurturing mother, to encourage her little boy not to become a carbon copy of his father. In essence, even though Baron will eventually profit from her husband's status of wealth, she should encourage him not to embrace his unscrupulous and self-absorbed character.

Just the other day, I heard a white man on TV declare that

Racism, Sexism, Trumpism, Pseudo-Christianity and the Cinema

Donald Trump is a "role model! What does that say about the spokesman? I just hope he's not a parent. Because if he perceives Trump to be a person that children should look up to and emulate, no wonder America's kids are in so much trouble!

Again, I implore parents to step up to the plate.

Almost daily we have young people resorting to suicide in this country and practically bi-weekly we are made to endure school house shootings carried out by fellow classmates.

Why are some children so forlorn and hopeless and, others, so filled with hate and vile? It calls to mind something that the Christ said when He was carrying His cross to Calvary. I'm certain I can't quote His words in verbatim, but He informed His sympathizers, "Do not weep for me, weep for yourselves. For the time will come when they'll say blessed are the barren, blessed is the womb that never bore a child."

I can't avoid wondering if that's where we are today. Far too many parents are burying their children in this nation and far too many kids are contemptuous of their respective parents or consider them unimportant. And why? Again, I say parents are shirking their responsibilities.

Call me judgmental or even an "uppity nigger," I don't really care, but, seemingly, many, many parents are not fulfilling their loving or guidance roles. (And when you point to the POTUS as a role-model, you are probably not up to the task anyhow). But it takes a real parent, a genuine parent to yield his or her child a firm foundation.

There are certain facts children should be apprised of at home, prior to allowing them to face the world at-large. To their personal disenchantment, kids should be told that evil, just like good, very much exists in this world. Moreover, there are "good" people and there are "bad" people who they will eventually come to know (and, sorrowfully, the latter oftentimes outnumber the former). Tell them, too (and I realize parents balk at saying it), that everybody is not going to love or even like them. Caution them not to personalize that revelation. After all, a man called "Jesus" was hated by quite a few people and He was considered void of sin. But I'm reflecting on the above in behalf of kids who are subjected to bullying, and expressly the ones who are so depressed and hopeless that they consider taking their own lives.

I am keenly aware that they're too young to be discerning, but upon encouraging your offspring to be "nice, courteous and caring" themselves, tell them to try to avoid caustic and mean-spirited people also. (And people, basically, don't change much in this life. If they are mean and unpleasant as adults, they were the same way when they were kids). And when your child scopes out individuals who fit that pre-described bill, then suggest that they hastily move on and seek out more kind and virtue-minded people.

There are quite a few of those types of people in this world also (loving and compassionate individuals), but youngsters will not encounter them if they don't take the time to look for them. Absolutely nothing stays the same forever.

And I feel compelled to add this also, something that's quite personal to me. Sadly, I knew a couple of young men who died at their own hands, and their respective mothers never, ever stopped mourning their demises. Those moms, in fact, carried that heavy grief to their own graves. However, I imagine that's how all parents feel (mothers and fathers too) when they are made to funeralize and bury their children.

Although my heart goes out to suicidal children and their parents too, I don't know how to feel about murderous youngsters; neither the ones involved in schoolhouse massacres or inner-city shootings either. I perceive them as evil-incarnated and devil-inspired, but, admittedly, that's my anger and despair talking. What could be in those kid's sick minds?

Then again, I can't help wondering about their select parents either. What is their story, and especially the fathers and mothers of all the Caucasian shooters? I do not like reducing the issue to race, but when I hear that the "guilty" shooter "was affiliated with

Racism, Sexism, Trumpism, Pseudo-Christianity and the Cinema

some white hate faction, I soon switch my focus to their parents. Unless they are, somehow, influenced or coerced by principal (not principled) adults in their young lives, where do they contract that kind of racist mind-set? If their in-house parents aren't the supreme source of such ugly biasness, then, maybe, that white spokesman on my television was right on target. To some Caucasian citizens, Donald J. Trump is a heralded role-model! Therefore, when white parents and guardians hear their children engage in regular, mean-spirited name-calling; when they call black NFL players "sons-of-bitches," when they refer to struggling, poverty-stricken nations as "shit-hole countries," when they brand Mexicans and immigrants "rapists" and "dogs," when they boast of "grabbing women by their genitals", when they sanction police officers behaving as "judge, jury and executioners" while performing their jobs, when they call for the "incarceration of a long-time public servant," when they discredit the free press, calling it "fake news," and when they comfortably lie faster than a dog can trot, then bystanding parents can tip their hats to President Donald Trump. They can rest assured that their child will be in good hands–but, please, make sure that the subject child is male, not female.

Pseudo Christianity

"I implore you to follow me as I follow Jesus Christ. If I choose to embark on another road, thereby detouring from the Lord's righteous path, then stop following me!"

In Search of True Christianity

Several months ago, a Nigerian friend of mine made a remark that gave me momentary pause. We were conversing about racism in America and she said, "I think God Himself is a racist." I was curious and I immediately asked her to expound on her rather odd statement. Without hesitation, she remarked, "If He wasn't a racist–then He would have made all people the same, exact color." Right away, I replied, "If it wasn't skin color, people would find some other 'stand-out' trait to fuel their discrimination. Let's face it, people love looking down on other people."

I issued that simplistic response but afterwards, when I was by my lonesome, I thought more intently about my friend's declaration and viewed it from a different angle.

I thought about all the Caucasian people who proudly consider themselves "Christians" and emerged with a rather provocative supposition. Keeping the Supreme Being well in mind, I wondered if He, to some degree, focuses on the ever-present racial disparity issue when passing judgment on the lifelong actions of mankind. My grandmother truly believed it is one of the Lord's guidelines used in 'separating the lambs from the goats.'

Plainly stated, a person cannot honestly adorn himself in a

Racism, Sexism, Trumpism, Pseudo-Christianity and the Cinema

Christian cloak if he (or she) hates for the mere sake of skin-pigmentation. Also, if my recollection is generally correct, God, Himself posed a query in the Holy Bible that asks,

"How can you claim you love Me, whom you have not seen, and hate thy neighbor, whom you have seen?" That acutely resonates with me because I've lived my life, well-entrenched in my personal assessment of Christianity. To be a true Christian is to be truly Christ-like! That does not mean that a person should walk on water, turn water into wine, restore sight to blind men or bring life back to the dead either. It means feeding the hungry, administering to the sick and treating other people like you, yourself, wish to be treated. I am not a preacher or a saint, but I do know a bonafide Christian when I encounter one. And to my great regret, I have observed very few of them during my lifetime.

Personally speaking, if I was hard-pressed to pinpoint a "Christian" in my life, without hesitation I would gladly cite my "Uncle Bill," a man who was married to my mother's older sister. In the wake of my father's gradual departure from my life and the, simultaneous, death of his own beloved wife, my uncle selflessly offered shelter to me, my quartet of brothers and my mother as well. In spite of having five children of his own, he welcomed my family into his residence, helped feed and sustain us and provided the stability we so desperately needed.

But that was hardly the full extent of my uncle's overt generosity and compassionate spirit. Owning a three-storied house, he also took in his invalid dad, his fraternal twin sister, an additional sister-in-law and a young relocating niece over the years. And, commendably too, the man did all of the forementioned while actively working two (2) eight-hour jobs and faithfully attending church services each and every Sunday.

Although I'd be the first to admit that individuals like my beloved uncle comes along once in a blue moon (I tried my best to emulate him, but I'm afraid I fell short), but I do not believe a person (a man or a woman) has to be virtually superhuman to reach Christian status, or become Christ-like. Admittedly, it may be difficult and, sometimes, dispiriting, but it's wholly reachable. Notably though, if insincerity and hypocrisy is thrown into the equation, it'll be a waste of energy. It would be like assembling a pocket watch with a sledgehammer.

To my utter amazement, despite any concrete or verifying evidence whatsoever, there has always been an inordinate number of Caucasian people in this country who actually regard themselves as Christians. It's an exasperating and puzzling phenomenon to me!

Throughout their history, Caucasians have audaciously deemed themselves as Christians, and so many of them still do. When they waged war on Native Americans (killing them, slaughtering the buffalo and even giving them small pox-infested blankets), they perceived themselves as Christians. When they flagrantly stole Africans from their motherland (enslaving them, emasculating them and burning and hanging them too), they called themselves Christians. And even at present, while millions of them bask in the racist sunlight of the Donald Trump administration, they pride themselves in being Christians. As absurd and grievous as it sounds, even the KKK (Ku Klux Klan) has always viewed itself as a Christian organization. In addition, even the white men who viciously murdered and mutilated Emmett Till way back in the 1950's regarded themselves as Christians. And the list goes on and on and on.

However, I leave all of those delusionary hypocrites to themselves. I believe there's a higher authority in the picture and I firmly believe, also, that people (regardless of their skin color) reap what they sow. Therefore, in knowing that evil has a reckoning in itself, I am resigned to avoiding as many pseudo and self-proclaimed "Christians" as humanly possible. For they are a total vexation to my spirit!

As I alluded to, however, Caucasian people are not the only racial group who gives Christianity and religion a soiled and bad

Racism, Sexism, Trumpism, Pseudo-Christianity and the Cinema

reputation. My own people, fellow Afro-Americans, are oftentimes guilty of doing likewise. But to their credit, their defamation is seldom embroidered in racism. Instead, it frequently involves over-zealousness and fanaticism. I could pen a 1,000-page book about the subject but, for the time being, I'd like to cite a few of the relevant experiences I personally dealt with along life's road. I still marvel in light of some of them.

First off, after starting off as a Baptist, I delved into the Pentecostal faith later on in my life.

In fact, I eventually took a Pentecostal bride and married her in her home church. I emphasized "her" church because I was attending an entirely different Pentecostal church prior to getting married.

Notably, the memories that I'm on the verge of disclosing occurred before I was wedded, and even prior to becoming engaged also. In fact, I was only sporadically dating in those days.

I don't know how much the average person knows about the Pentecostal faith but I don't think it is like any other religious faction. It is noisy (replete with singing and musical instruments), it's spirited (everything from dancing and racing around in the church building) and it is exuberant with frequent prophesizing and boisterous outcries of hallelujah. In addition, those in attendance (the members, especially) are encouraged to give vocal testimonies and to actively engage in something called "tarrying for the Holy Ghost." In translation, it means pleading to be saved.

Admittedly, from the very beginning, I was a mite skeptical of some of the church goings-on. I wasn't quite convinced that the attending people were really "in the spirit" when they proceeded to sprint around the church or when they "passed out" (fainted) in a state of religious euphoria either.

All in all, everything was going fine with my church affiliation, that is until two fellow members took a marked interest in me. One of them was an elderly black woman whom I'll refer to as 'Mother Emma' and the other individual was a young white lady who formerly was married to a black man. In addition, the latter had two biracial kids. I'll call her 'Angie.'

Seemingly, since I was a single male, Angie was romantically-inclined in her interest in me while Mother Emma was seemingly concerned with my salvation. To be honest, I was not thrilled with either one of them.

I realized that Mother Emma meant well, and I basically liked her, but she eventually got on my last nerve.

That's because every given Sunday, prior to church services, she sought me out to give me an "urgent" message. She started off, saying, "Brother L, Brother L" (that, of course, was me), "the Lord told me to tell you that you need to become more involved in the church. I think He wants you to become a deacon."

I calmly responded, taking the elderly lady's advisement in stride and simply said, "Thanks, Mother Emma,

I'll take some time and consider what you said." Then, the very next Sunday morning and, again, before services got underway, she came to me with, yet, another message.

In a whispering tone, she stated, "Brother L, the Lord told me to tell you that if you stop drinking beer, you'll get the Holy Ghost."

Again, I graciously thanked Mother Emma for her message and soon walked away. I wasn't remotely upset with my elderly friend. In fact, I was somewhat tickled shortly afterwards. It was because I imagined asking Mother Emma to obtain the upcoming 'Lotto' numbers from the Lord. Now that would have been a heads-up I could rejoice over.

Even in the wake of my innate sense of humor, I slowly became more and more weary of Mother Emma's unsolicited advice, and especially since it was secondhand from the lips of Jesus (or God). I even came up with the idea of arriving at church after the services officially began, thinking that would somehow derail Mother Emma's message process. It did not, however, work. On the third Sunday, the old lady approached me after church ended.

Racism, Sexism, Trumpism, Pseudo-Christianity and the Cinema

"Brother L, Brother L," she joyously stated, "the Lord told me to tell you that if you come to Wednesday night's services and tarry for the Holy Ghost, He will give it to you." I nodded my head in appreciation and even mouthed,

"Thanks again, Mother Emma." However, I could not wait to get home on that particular afternoon and go to my fridge and grab a cold can of beer. I sat, watching television and I thought, "This is not right! A guy shouldn't go to church on Sunday mornings and then come back home feeling depressed in the afternoon. I don't know how I'm gonna do it, but I'm gonna put a stop to this."

On the fourth Sunday I arrived at church prior to the start of services. I, both, dreaded and looked forward to seeing Mother Emma. She approached me and, just like clockwork, verbally opened up with her usual salutation.

"Brother L–Brother L" she excitedly uttered. Charge me with disrespect and rudeness if you wish, but I abruptly interrupted my adviser. "Mother Emma, are you going to tell me something that the Lord told you to pass on to me?" I asked, surprising her. "Yeah, He told me."

I cut Mother Emma off once again as I retrieved a folded, pre-written note from my shirt pocket. "Here–I want to give this to you," I told her.

"What is this?" Mother Emma asked as she grimacingly grasped the note.

"Written on there is my home telephone number and my address," I sternly explained.

"If the Lord wants to get in touch with me, please tell Him to write me a letter or call me on my phone. I am really tired of Him telling you stuff about me. Mother Emma, I haven't done anything so horrible that warrants God not speaking to me. I may not have the Holy Ghost, but I'm always trying to do right and live a Christian life. Plus, I've been baptized twice.

Do you know" how" I feel when you tell me that God chooses

not to speak to me? Mother Emma, I should not have to come to church happy and return home feeling sad as hell.

And that's how I feel sometimes."

Admittedly, it was a little icy between me and Mother Emma after the note incident. But we eventually made up and remained cordial throughout the period I stayed at that church.

I left for good approximately four months later. Notably, I was granted the Holy Ghost before I made my departure, but at a different Pentecostal church.

I never knew who provided the young white girl, Angie, my home telephone number (maybe, Mother Emma), but she got into the habit of calling me quite frequently. After a while, she professed being attracted to me and then asked if I had mutual feelings for her. I did not and I gingerly tried to convey to her why. I even took the initiative to cite an old-time song, hoping it would, somehow, soften the rejection.

"From time to time," I told her, "I've had friends ask me if I'd ever consider marrying a white woman. And everytime I'd recite the lyrics of this song. 'I want a girl, just like the girl–who married dear old dad.' Now, dad wasn't so dear, but my mom certainly was. And I'm afraid I still feel that way."

Angie's counter response was,

"But, who's talking about marriage?"

I really didn't know how to reply to my admirer's foregoing words, so I decided to speak candidly. I told her my reluctance wasn't because she was unattractive or unappealing to me, telling her, too, that she could look like Liz Taylor and even that wouldn't influence me. Right or wrong (and possibly the latter), I confessed I was too hung up on history, I was privy to too many well-documented, true-life cases that involved lying Caucasian females, racist blood-thirsty white men and helpless and, often times, innocent black victims.

Angie, of course, had nothing to do with any of those yesteryear atrocities or miscarriages of justice but I could not help how I

Racism, Sexism, Trumpism, Pseudo-Christianity and the Cinema

was frequently haunted by them. Even today the gross injustice surrounding those long-ago accounts still plague me.

Although I came to regard my interactions with, both, Mother Emma and Angie as awkward and somewhat anguish-ridden, I found myself becoming more and more disenchanted with the church itself. Admittedly, I was a novice when it came to the Pentecostal faith but even prior to being considered 'saved,' I felt there was something seriously awry with it. In the back of my mind, I only hoped it was the church, not the faith in itself.

Starting with the top, the young pastor (whom I'll call 'Rev. Ellis'), and I seemed to have personalities that did not mesh. Maybe, because he was 27 years old and married with two kids and I was 32 and single with no children, we had no common ground. Maybe. Then again, since he hailed from the deep south and I was a street-wise, big-city guy, that, too, might have put us on different levels. However, if I was pressed to put my finger on the major quality that addressed our persistent disconnect, I would have to point to joviality.

As I indicated earlier, I am almost a perennial jokester and the young preacher seemed totally void of a sense of humor. In fact, he came across as virtually too-serious and that was particularly bothersome to me. I perceived him as an enigma.

However, I was deftly comfortable with my light-heartedness and my jovial nature and I, therefore, did not allow the pastor's ultra-pious behavior to affect me. Not only did I continue kidding around while interacting with my fellow churchgoers, there were occasions when I joked around with the good reverend himself.

For example, one Saturday afternoon the entire church congregation was enjoying a picnic out in a Saint Louis county park. We had been there a couple of hours, everybody seemed to be enjoying themselves, and I took a few moments to share some pleasantries with Rev. Ellis. We were both smiling at the time, we even cordially shook hands and then the 'Rev'. asked me if I was having a good time.

"Oh, I've been having a wonderful time," I replied, still grinning, "good food, good company, fun all around, but I've been searching for it all day long and I can't seem to find it."

Immediately, the pastor became visually sedate. "What have you been looking for, Brother L?" he quizzed. "Maybe, I can assist you in locating it."

"You know, Rev.," I responded, pretending to be serious myself. "I've been looking for the darn beer keg ever since I got here. Did you guys forget to bring it out, or what? And I don't mind going back to grab it."

From the minister's facial expression, any bystanding observer would have thought the man was suddenly stricken. He opted to put a 'comforting' hand on my shoulder, softly saying,

"We're gonna have to seriously pray for you, Brother L. Please come up to the altar tomorrow morning. Please do that for me?" I stood, shaking my head in amazement and, almost, hopelessness.

"Rev. Ellis, you need to lighten up, my man, I spoke, facing the preacher head-on. "I well know alcohol is not allowed or welcomed at church picnics, especially Pentecostal picnics. Man, I was just joking!"

I was on the threshold of telling the pastor that I couldn't wait to get home after the picnic, to have a beer. I wanted to tell him he was 'driving me to drink,' but I elected not to. I walked away, however, surmising that it was he, the good Reverend, who told Mother Emma I was an avid beer drinker. After all, it wasn't like I walked around carrying a can of beer or wearing a Budweiser tee-shirt. Otherwise, unless the Lord actually spoke to her, how did Mother Emma know about my fondness for beer? I wish I could report that all of my interactions with the churches' pastor was relatively smooth and light, but I cannot. On the contrary, since I periodically took issue with some of the goings-on in the church, he and I would occasionally lock horns. I wasn't trying to take over his church or be a wisenheimer, but when he encouraged the congregation to not only refrain from

Racism, Sexism, Trumpism, Pseudo-Christianity and the Cinema

watching television, but to discard their TV's altogether, I opted to speak to him about it.

Initially, when Rev. Ellis voiced that novel policy from behind his pulpit, I let it go in one ear and out the other. And that's exactly what I did when the pastor and his die-hard followers attached sinfulness to simply seeing a picture show also. But when it became clear to me that the greater majority of the congregation was actually obeying his orders, I discreetly challenged him. Naturally, he didn't appreciate an "upstart" like me questioning his God-inspired mission and he accused me of wanting to remain "in the world." I took staunch issue with that assessment also.

"Rev. Ellis, you may take refuge from not being in the world," I responded, "but still you should be aware of what's going on in the world. I talk to people in the congregation, and they don't know anything. I'm not being overly critical, but they are plainly ignorant. And in the truest definition of the world. They don't know anything–except what's in the Bible. And you sure can't talk about it 24-7."

"Maybe, you can't talk about it? Brother L," the reverend countered. "The Holy Bible has everything in it that people need to know and talk about. It's the alpha and the omega, especially in my church. I think you should take time out and seriously think about that, Brother L. We love having you amongst us, but you're gonna have to decide if you're going to remain here."

I was greatly disillusioned when I left the pastor's study that particular day, but I had to admit Rev. Ellis had a valid point when he talked about me making a personal decision.

Since I wasn't a female, I had no opinion regarding women not wearing make-up or them wearing dresses only either.

But I was becoming more and more disenchanted with the churches' ideology (in actuality, the pastor's ideology) and I felt it was gradually embracing cultism. I could even imagine the majority of my fellow churchgoers drinking the poison-laced kool-aid.

Upon alluding to the "kool-aid" incident, I am compelled

to cite the infamous Guyana tragedy and its chief orchestrator, the charismatic but Satan-inspired Rev. Jim Jones. In duping and coercing a whole multitude of gullible and misery-laden people to perceive him as a prophet and supreme Christian, Jones methodically relocated his followers to a faraway, foreign land and, then, prodded them to collectively embrace self-destruction and out-and-out murder.

If there was such a thing as a "cultism playbook," I am certain a great deal of the forestated guidelines would be included in it. An egocentric leader, a fanatical and weak-minded audience (or base) and a burning desire to flee the modern world would surely be addressed in it. When people feel disenfranchised and are absent of hope, they are open to practically anything the diabolical Satan sends their way.

And upon revisiting the Guyana catastrophe, the Rev. Jim Jones was a zealous envoy.

Am I suggesting that Rev. Ellis was cut from the same cloth as the infamous Jim Jones?

No, Ellis didn't come across as sinister or a disciple of the devil. But, symbolically, he profited from a Jones-like tactic. While Ellis did not physically transport his flock to an entirely different locale, he indoctrinated them mentally. Establishing himself as an authoritative oracle, he, seemingly, controlled their thinking process.

Of course, that was my personal assessment and since the greater majority of the congregation did not remotely align themselves with my viewpoint (not that I polled them on it), I was on the verge of packing it in and leaving the church altogether. On a fateful Sunday morning little did I know that my departure would be dramatically accelerated.

Early, on a Sabbath morning I'd like to forget, and prior to church proceedings getting underway, Rev. Ellis had something very serious and pressing to share with the early arrivers. It was a revelation that involved Angie, who was our lone white church

Racism, Sexism, Trumpism, Pseudo-Christianity and the Cinema

member, and a thirty-something black man whom I'll call 'Deacon Clark.' The deacon was a personable young man I frequently associated with and had grown to like very much. Obviously, since Clark served in a deacon capacity, he was more spiritually-minded than I was.

Hopefully, I was spot on with that foregoing assessment because as circumstances unfolded, Clark dearly needed to be well-grounded in faith. From the very moment the pastor invoked his given name, my eyes were virtually fixated on the deacon.

Speaking as if he, himself, was eyewitness to his divulged verbal account, Rev. Ellis talked candidly about Deacon Clark's salacious misbehavior with a resistant, innocent and very vulnerable Angie. Calling it an 'attempted rape,' the pastor left no room for doubt and voiced no mercy whatsoever for the would-be rapist, Deacon Clark.

Furthermore, as tears rolled down the cheeks of the subdued and anguished Clark, Ellis told the congregation to "rebuke and shun the deacon entirely." In essence, he encouraged 'us' to neither speak nor look Clark's way. Completely ostracize him! And as loyal, obedient followers, they collectively behaved accordingly.

Maybe Clark, himself, was God-influenced because I don't know how he was able to even stay inside the church on that fateful morning and afternoon. He remained grievous, silent and stationary throughout the worship proceedings.

Although I entertained the notion to just get up and leave, I, too, remained on hand that day. However, it wasn't because I was particularly interested in what was going on around me. (I can't even recall what the main sermon was about that afternoon). Instead, I was sitting in my pew, quietly stewing. I kept dwelling on Deacon Clark's dilemma. I was aware that the Holy Bible advocates rebuking people in light of their respective sins. But I did not think an entire church was obligated to do it. Plus, if the sinner was sorry and repentive (and Clark certainly appeared to be just that), I thought forgiveness and mercy was very much in order. Moreover, I wondered if a mere man, clergyman or not, can rightfully pass judgment on another human being.

However, there was another level to my anxiety also. It centered around the accuser, Angie, and her apparent-defender, the churches' pastor. I recalled a remark that Angie once shared with me, back in the days when she regularly telephoned me. It may have been completely innocent on the reverend's part, but she claimed he encouraged her to refrain from 'having her hair cut.' According to Angie (her precise words), Ellis said, "I love seeing white women's hair blowing in the wind."

Now, I never could wrap my head around what might have prompted the pastor to make such a flirtatious comment or why Angie elected to tell me about it either. Maybe she was lying through her teeth or, maybe, she was being truthful. And if she was, what did that say about Rev. Ellis? If he secretly had designs on Angie, did he even entertain the idea that she might be prevaricating about Deacon Clark? I was in a mental tizzy!

Finally, the services concluded on the fateful day I'm reliving. The congregational body actively began to file out the church, intent upon returning to their outlying homes. With me lingering around and yearning to converse with Deacon Clark and, therefore, bringing up the rear, it was one of the saddest and shameful sights I've ever been privy to.

As Deacon Clark stood near the walkway outside the church building, still heavily consumed by his inner grief (his face was still damp with tears), his fellow church members strolled pass him like he had leprosy. Stoically obeying their pastor's forestated commands, they neither spoke to the deacon or looked his way.

I, of course, was a dissenter. I had pre-planned what I was going to do and I knew exactly what I was going to say as well. With the pastor and his wife looking on, I opted to firmly embrace Clark, briskly shake his hand and issue a statement of encouragement and farewell to him.

"I know where you work, my man," I smilingly told him," and

Racism, Sexism, Trumpism, Pseudo-Christianity and the Cinema

I'll stop by to check you out from time to time. But, you can make book on this, I will never, ever set foot in this church again. So, you take care of yourself and hang in there. It's been a real pleasure knowing you and I'll truly miss you."

Deacon Clark declared he would miss me also and with that said, we bided goodbye. I did occasionally visit him at his work place but just as I vowed, I never entered that Pentecostal church again. I'm sorry to say it but I left there with few regrets.

To be perfectly honest, I never found out if Deacon Clark was guilty as charged by Angie and Rev. Ellis or not.

I never understood why the churches' pastor was so hell-bent on publicly chastising and humiliating the deacon either. Even upon retreating from the church that day, I had a series of relevant questions swirling through my mind. Such as:

Was the assault reported to the police? If so, was Clark placed under arrest? Where and when did the incident take place?

Were there any witnesses to the episode?

Notably, Angie's two kids lived under her roof. Therefore, if it transpired in her home, were they made to suffer through such an unsavory happening?

Furthermore, did the minister, acting as jury and judge, take out time to listen to Clark's version of the story? Then again, if the deacon accepted blame and was as remorseful of his conduct as he appeared to be in the short aftermath of it, why was Rev. Ellis so strongly inclined to openly rebuke him? Exactly, what was in the pastor's mind?

Due to the fact that Clark was black and Angie was white, did that, in some way, affect his feelings? For sure, the minister was an Afro-American male himself but, upon recalling Angie's "hair blowing in the wind" tale, I was somewhat suspicious of his innermost motives. But frankly speaking, since I did not know the definitive answers to any of the forementioned questions, I was leery of the entire affair.

Speaking of affairs, in the aftermath of my severing ties with my former place of worship, I was told that Rev. Ellis engaged in one of his very own. In addition, it subsequently ended his marriage. Whenever I'm apprised of any marital break-up, my heart automatically goes out to children who are, alternately, hurt and affected. Therefore, my sympathy went out to Mrs. Ellis and her two young kids. However, I could not help wondering if the pastor opted to instruct his flock to rebuke and ostracize him in light of his unfaithfulness. Or, was his personal sinful behavior more palatable—and tolerable to him?

Wolves Dressed in Sheep's Clothing

Leave it to humankind to take something that should be regarded as beautiful and uplifting and, subsequently, render it dispiriting and anguish-filled. Sorrowfully, I'm focusing on the act of attending church services itself. People may disagree with me on any level they like, but I've always believed that churchgoing is not only sacred, it is synonymous with great joy and inner-peace. With the desire to pay homage to a benevolent and merciful God, it is a set aside period for fellowshipping with like-minded individuals and sincerely wishing them all well. In an altruistic sense, it's a prime time for exuding love and selflessness.

Owing to the Supreme Being, Himself (or my innate stubbornness), I still cling to the foregoing philosophy.

However, over the years, it has become clear to me that my personal assessment of traditional churchgoing is not embraced by a large number of so-called "Christians". It is my hope, however, that the greater majority of churchgoers do embrace it.

Some readers of this book may very well accuse me of 'Loving to talk about myself,' but those folks would be essentially wrong. I'm a staunch believer in, both, "Fate" and "Karma." Therefore, I firmly maintain that people are predestined to experience every life happening that occurs and, in accordance to right or wrong-

Racism, Sexism, Trumpism, Pseudo-Christianity and the Cinema

headed choices, they are rewarded or punished for their actions at a later date.

So, instead of concentrating on the misadventures and exploits of other individuals, and instead of surmising what those individuals might think about certain topics, I opt to inject myself into situations as a kind of prototype (an 'everyman,' if you will). And by inserting myself into various episodic situations, I am able to divulge my perspective and viewpoints. I host very few inhibitions and secrets.

With that stated, I would like to revisit a conversation I once had with a Nigerian friend of mine. After calling God a racist, she argued that God should have made all people the same color. Based on that premise, she felt racism would be nonexistent. I totally disagreed with her. In verbatim, I declared, "If it wasn't skin color, people would find some other physical trait to fuel their discrimination." Additionally, I told her that people loved looking down on other people.

Call it an idiosyncrasy on my part, a quirk or whatever, but I've always disliked wearing neckties. Even as a soldier in the United States Army, I strongly objected to wearing ties. I've even jovially rationalized my stance, telling people why I'm opposed to wearing them. It's simply because I was hanged in my first life. But all kidding aside, I never guessed that such a small dress adornment, a necktie, could invoke a feeling of intense resentment in some people.

As I maintained previously, everything in life happens for a reason and, therefore, after I promised to attend church services in the city of Chicago, Illinois and my back began to severely ache, that occurrence, too, had its purpose. That spontaneous ailment, paired with my steadfast determination to fulfill my earlier vow found me at a large, popular church on a particular Sunday morning in the renown Windy City. Noticeably slumped over and enduring horrendous back agony (at the age of 33, I'm sure I resembled a 90-year old man), I gingerly climbed the churches front steps and slowly walked inside the sanctuary.

To say that the church was crowded would be a gross understatement. It was packed to the very hilt! And since my friend (a native Chicagoan) and I were late arrivers, there were no available seats to be found. To my greatest regret, we were obliged to advance further inside the church and then stand alongside a wall.

My body was practically wracked with severe pain but, still, I was determined to endure. It was at that point, as I opted to raise my head to take a kind of panoramic view of the church itself, that it dawned on me that I was being visually scrutinized. I was certain that my facial expression was indicative of how I felt physically and mentally. I was perspiring and even feeling somewhat feverish.

However, the eyes that were trained on me were not denoting sympathy or any degree of empathy. They were, instead, hostile and collectively resentful. Then it dawned on me. I was not wearing a necktie! Additionally, I wasn't attired in a suit either!

I, soon, looked around and virtually every man I observed, including my friend who chided me for not wearing a tie, was dressed in attractive suits; replete with neckties and all the accessories. Then, when it came to the female churchgoers, they were garbed immaculately, also. Many of them, along with a variety of hats, were adorned in expensive looking dresses, glistening jewelry and even fur coats. It was like being in the middle of an extravagant fashion show.

Therefore, I really should not have been in their luxurious presence! (At least, those were the vibes I was feeling). Seemingly, the entire congregation regarded themselves as royalty and to them I was but a lowly pauper. I imagined they were thinking: "How dare he invade our elitist domain, boldly void of a tie and suit! Who the hell does he think he is? He's got his nerve!"

In reality, no one actually mouthed the foregoing words (I'm just being melodramatic) but the condemnation in the eyes of many of them spoke volumes. Although they looked down their noses at me for violating their dress code (being absent of a suit

Racism, Sexism, Trumpism, Pseudo-Christianity and the Cinema

and necktie), one would think I was buck naked in their eyesight. But what struck me was this: As I remained practically glued to that wall throughout the duration of the church proceedings, aching and looking like death warmed over, not a one of them, neither male nor female, displayed one iota of human sympathy towards me.

I recall thinking, if I was seated in that overcrowded sanctuary and I observed an individual in my condition, I would have insisted that he or she take my seat. I know me, and I am positive I would have done just that. Because, in my opinion, it would have been the "Christian" thing to do.

Looking back, I regard the entire episode as stupid, shameful and revealing. If anyone had even hinted to those church-goers in attendance that day that they were not Christians, I believe they would have been fighting mad. As I shook them off later that afternoon, I only wished they had observed the incident through my eyes. And what I saw was a bunch of well-dressed hypocrites who were so into themselves, it rendered them dispassionate and pompous. God, please save me from the so-called good people and the pseudo Christians in this world!

In retrospect, whenever I relive that church happening that took place in the 1970s, I, again, find myself reflecting on that assertion made by my African friend in 2017.

Upon branding God a racist for not painting all humankind the same, exact color, she and I agreed to disagree. Although I appreciated my friend's frustration and her craving for fair play as well, I argued that, if it wasn't skin color, mankind would find another trait (or 'difference', such as a necktie) to fixate their hatred on. And, tragically, all one has to do is to look back upon history, specifically at the Germans and the Jewish people during World War II. Some folks might consider me paranoid after mulling over my account of what transpired at that Chicago church.

They might even say I'm exaggerating. After all, the entire congregation wasn't acting snooty and snobbish. And there is a glimmer of truth in each of those assertions. Admittedly though, I have visited a slew of prominent cities in my lifetime and, seemingly, most of them have one or two highly-regarded and upper crust worship sites.

And while there's nothing wrong with attending churches of striking beauty and enormous splendor, and nothing wrong in being a proud member of that subject church either, there is something grossly amiss when an individual deems themselves exultant and elitist solely because of it.

Once, in the middle of a special religious celebration, an elderly Afro-American woman felt it was necessary and most appropriate to haughtily inform me that, "I and my family are longtime members of the SEWING-SO Church." Then, she turned right around and asked,

"Who are your people, young man, and what church do they regularly attend?"

My sense of humor is practically always on the tip of my tongue. I smilingly replied, saying,

"All I know, Ma'am, is that my people are black, a lot of them were once slaves and I'm afraid some of them are heathens. Some of them don't attend church at all."

"Oh–you're a kidder, aren't you?" The lady laughingly remarked.

"Yes, Ma'am, I do like to joke around," I admitted.

Jest can't help myself."

In all seriousness, and upon deleting the humor aspect altogether, I'm aware that people, in general, are desirous of outshining other people. Some of them are virtually obsessed with being the out-front drum-major instead of a member of the marching band. But an upstanding and honorable individual takes steps to earn such a stellar position. They don't trample over others to secure it or resort to bullying tactics in hot pursuit of it. And they don't take a page from Donald Trump's playbook by belittling and brow-beating competitors who are individuals with similar ambitions.

Racism, Sexism, Trumpism, Pseudo-Christianity and the Cinema

In essence, a person does not have to be wealthy, he or she does not have to be well-educated, they do not have to obtain celebrity-status, and one does not have to align her or himself with any grandiose institution or organization to achieve prominence or notoriety.

As Dr. Martin Luther King so eloquently suggested (and once again I'm paraphrasing), "If you want to be significant, if you want to be great, if you want to be first–then be first in love, be first in generosity, and all of the other shallow things do not matter.

In addition, Reverend King went on to contend that, "He who is greatest amongst you is he who serves." And King was expressly advocating serving "others" (humankind, in general), not yourself and certainly not people who exclusively share racial identity and heritage with you. If a man's compassion and love does not transcend skin color, then his heart is not right anyhow.

Furthermore, in concert with Dr. King's forestated philosophy, an individual does not have to be within the confines of an organized or even disorganized house of worship to approach a kind of greatest. A person can simply be in his or her home, in their respective work place, in a regular supermarket, in a club or bar, and even on a city street and still be a dedicated servant to God. And that, to me, is not only good news, it's great news! It clearly means an everyday person can secure a measure of greatness.

Admittedly, the forthcoming has been a lingering and lifelong mystery to me! I know it is widespread with bold hypocrisy and unmitigated mendacity, but if an individual is genuine in his or her pursuit of Christian status, when they feel secure upon achieving that sought-after goal, why do so many of them, then, go completely overboard with it? To me, it is like struggling to climb an ultra-steep hill, and after reaching the peak, you stumble and roll head-over-heels back down the other side. The exhaustive climb then becomes moot.

Seemingly, upon altogether displacing their own past missteps and indiscretions (some of them, quite sinful), the "newly-born"

Christian becomes surrogate preachers and flesh and blood saints. In a certain sense, they stand erect at the apex of that symbolic hill and begin to hurl rocks down at the other climbers.

I'm not suggesting that neophyte Christians should stay silent or closed-mouthed after reaching their aspired goal, I'm just cautioning, or imploring, them to shy away from becoming haughty, judgmental and self-righteous. Although it's really a world problem, Christianity and every other religion should not be elitist, divisive or provocative in nature. Instead, they should be intent and anchored in bringing mankind closer together.

Of course, the foregoing is one of the downsides surrounding the pursuit of Christianity and maybe the most prominent one also. But, unfortunately, there are other downers and one of them epitomizes pure fanaticism, as well as a lack of plain-old common sense. And, to one of my greatest regrets, I was personally made to deal with that particular downside when I served in the capacity of a business-manager for the Saint Louis public schools district.

In the early 1980s I was somewhat taken aback to learn that one of the school's teachers, despite being a traditional academic instructor, had taken the initiative to actively recruit and form a "gospel singing group," selecting students from her respective business classes. That, in itself, was unprecedented (and unheard of also), but since the school's principal officially sanctioned the venture, I was compelled to go along with it all. (By the way, the principal at that time was the same Caucasian boss I had when I filed that racial discrimination complaint with the Equal Employment Opportunities Commission).

The teacher involved (whom I'll call Ms. Cline) was, of course, an Afro-American woman and just so happened she was Pentecostal also.

With her serving as chief organizer and choir director too, she gradually molded the teen-aged group (all of them, black) into a talented and melodious gospel singing ensemble. And as time went

Racism, Sexism, Trumpism, Pseudo-Christianity and the Cinema

on, with numerous rehearsals under their belts, they would have been stiff competition for any gospel choir in the St. Louis region.

However, I wasn't alone in my praise for that student chorus. Ms. Cline, who diligently worked to enhance and polish the group's overall performance was well-pleased with her creation as well. In fact, she was so thrilled with her choir's prowess that she longed to share them with others. And upon acting on that desire, she obtained permission from the principal and booked the entire ensemble for an engagement outside the school. Specifically, she arranged for them to take the stage at Worlds of Fun. in Kansas City, Missouri. It was located approximately three hundred miles from St. Louis proper.

Although I was never sold on the idea of having an in-house gospel choir at our school, I was actually happy when I was informed of Ms. Cline's plan to take the group out of town. Since the kids were all black and I realized that some of them had never even been outside the city of Saint Louis, I began looking forward to the trip myself. I wasn't accompanying them on it but, nevertheless, I was joyous for them.

I wish I could report that it was smooth-sailing from that particular point on but I cannot. Even in the midst of my self-contained delight, I was somewhat wary of the entire undertaking. In actuality, there were so many things that could go wrong and so many relevant questions that loomed in the shadows.

As the school's treasurer, I was in charge of money matters and all the official paper work that would, alternately, make the pending trip a reality. And with 30 teenaged students (who comprised the choir) and a single teacher (Ms. Cline) as the slated travelers, it was not an easy task.

After obtaining written permission from the parents of each student, the participants, under the guidance of Ms. Cline, were assigned the chore of raising funds to finance the venture. And with modest donations from parents and guardians, along with the assorted fundraisers, it was an ongoing effort.

Lionel Barry Harris

In my personal viewpoint, the logistics were relatively simple: It was a three-day trip (from Friday through Sunday), it would require bus or train transportation to and from Kansas City, it was necessary to secure lodging arrangements for 32 people (the choir members, the teacher and, probably, the bus driver) and we were also obligated to purchase 'visitor' tickets for the Worlds of Fun amusement park.

Well, it should have been simple, but it was not! After negotiating a lodging contract with a prominent hotel chain in K.C., I sat back, waiting for the stipulated funds to come my way. After all, in spite of my personal frets, Ms. Cline was the conduit of those monies and she, essentially, was running the whole show.

Maybe, I'm a born worrier or I allow pessimism to, sometimes, seep into my mind, but I secretly wondered if Ms. Cline honestly considered what she was doing. I could not refrain from posing a series of questions to myself.

Such as: Since the choir was comprised of 30 teenagers (both girls and boys), how could Ms. Cline, a single individual, properly chaperone them? To me, that was a mammoth task in itself and since the teacher was unmarried and had no children of her own as well, I foresaw big problems, if not disaster!

In addition, I wondered why the school's principal, who gave the green light to the entire endeavor, didn't entertain similar thoughts. I knew Ms. Cline was well-entrenched in her faith, but was the principal, himself, somehow influenced by her religious fervor? The man seemed to be "all-in" with the impending trek and I wondered what was he thinking! I tried to stay calm and I tried to remain on the sidelines too, but I was highly skeptical of all of it.

As things pressed on, I tried my hardest to put the upcoming choir excursion on the back-burner. After all, it was six weeks away and I had not, yet, seen one red cent aimed at financing it. Then, all of a sudden, strange things started to occur.

For instance: Since I was the official check writer,

Ms. Cline would turn over the raised monies to me, I would

Racism, Sexism, Trumpism, Pseudo-Christianity and the Cinema

place it in a special school account I set up for the undertaking, and I would, then, deposit the funds (along with other monies) into the bank. That was standard operational procedures—but it was not SOP for a teacher to deposit monies with me one day, request that I write a check for the entire sum the very next day and have a zero balance in the account afterwards. And that, to a tee, describes Ms. Cline's inter actions with me. To be specific, she would hand over a thousand dollars to me on a Tuesday afternoon and instruct me to send a check for the sum total to the Kansas City hotel on the very next morning, Wednesday. It was rather unorthodox and I didn't much like it, but I went along with it anyhow.

The red flag went up after I paid off the hotel bill in its entirety (per the negotiated contract) and prior to me emptying out the choir account once again by purchasing Worlds of Fun admission tickets for each participant. It was at that juncture that I addressed an important query to Ms. Cline and received a very unexpected and rather bizarre answer.

With absolutely no money in the choir account (another zero balance), I asked her, "What about the transportation to Kansas City and back? How are you guys gonna get there?" Not missing a beat, Ms. Cline casually replied,

"The Lord will provide."

I was instantly taken aback and I initially thought the teacher was kidding, but she wasn't. She looked markedly serious and she was not smiling. Ordinarily, I would have taken issue with the woman's reply but since I knew she was Pentecostal and realized, too, that a kind of fanaticism sometimes existed in that faith, I didn't think I could reason with her. However, I talked myself into posing the transportation question to her several other times anyhow and, sadly, was given the same, odd answer.

"The Lord will provide."

Naturally, I was alarmed by the teacher's rather curt response and I had no other recourse than to apprise the principal of that reply. Then, when I initially approached the man, telling him about

Ms. Cline's response in verbatim, he also voiced a very asinine remark.

"Well, I'm letting Ms. Cline handle everything," he flippantly stated. "It's her baby and she says she's got everything under control. I take her at her word."

I tried to assure the principal that the woman did not have things under control, especially, when it came to the transportation aspect, but my words fell on deaf ears. I left the administrator's office, shaking my head in frustration.

During that man-to-man meeting with my boss, I also referred to the contract we had forged with the hotel in K.C. I told him it stipulated that if we (the school) failed to cancel the reservation prior to two (2) weeks of the check-in day, we're compelled to forfeit half of the funds that we paid to them. That, too, went into one of the principal's ears and came out the other one.

But I refused to give up. Twice during the week prior to the hotel deadline, I approached Ms. Cline and the principal too. And to my utter dismay, they both recycled their previous verbal reactions. The teacher once again invoked, "The Lord will provide" and the principal expressed his confidence in Ms. Cline. Again, he said, "I'm letting Ms. Cline handle everything."

The situation, was not only disturbing to me, it was vexing and downright bizarre. And since I was aware that there were no more fundraisers being conducted, I was severely exasperated.

Despite my personal reluctance regarding the trip, I could imagine what it meant to the kids involved and with that solely in mind, I became somewhat of a nuisance (if not, a pain in the butt) to, both, the in-charge teacher and the gullible, but colluding principal as well. Even after the hotel deadline had come and gone, I still approached and nagged that pair in regards to the transportation issue.

Finally, the long-awaited Friday arrived on the scene.

Early that morning the participating students entered the

Racism, Sexism, Trumpism, Pseudo-Christianity and the Cinema

school building, happily carrying their suitcases and bags and even sack lunches and assorted snacks, all in joyous anticipation of the upcoming out-of-town trip.

However, to my heavy sorrow and seething anger, too, the Lord did not provide, at least, not that day. There was no chartered bus and no other mode of transportation forthcoming. And to be on hand and observe those disenchanted teen agers, sitting around moping (along with being teased by non-participating classmates) was purely heartbreaking to me.

I was even tearful at one point. For I knew how many disappointments awaited those black kids in life itself, but this particular one was one they could (and should) have done without. Those young people did not deserve it and it was totally unfair to them.

However, in my opinion, it had nothing whatsoever to do with the Lord. Instead, it had everything to do with two zip damn fool adults, the choir director and the principal. I just hoped neither of them would say anything to me.

Unfortunately, though, one of them did opt to speak to me. It was the principal.

While displaying a face of frantic puzzlement, he posed "the" number one question to me that I felt should not have come from his stupid mouth. "Where's the bus?" he quizzed.

There was no one around us when the administrator addressed me (not that I really cared) but I was glad there wasn't. That's because I lost my cool and composure and I did not mince my words. "Why the hell are you even asking me that?" I responded. "There is no damn bus and I kept telling your ass that it wasn't! This is partially your fault!"

Of course, my boss was highly upset with me. "You have no right to speak to me like that!" he snapped, trying to chastise me. "I'm the Principal–and that's insubordination, plain as day!"

"Well–I'll tell you what," I proposed. "Why don't you bring me up on charges? Cause I'd love to tell the powers that be about your dumb ass! You knew Ms. Cline was a damn religious' fanatic, but you didn't give a care!

Man, git outta my face! Hey, and do what you wanna do."

At that juncture, I didn't wait for the Principal to "git outta my face," I proceeded to get out of his face. Still engulfed in anger, I immediately walked away from him. I, then, went back to my office, closed my door and sat silently at my desk. I willed myself to calm down and relax.

Although I was later told that Ms. Cline drove to the not-too-distant Greyhound Bus station on the day of the fiasco, trying frantically to charter a bus at the last minute, but it was obviously fruitless. She did not have adequate funds, there were no bus drivers available and even if there was one, he would have also required weekend lodging arrangements.

When I finally emerged from my office around two P.M. that afternoon, I was just in time to view a bunch of disheartened choir members as they departed the school building. With their bags and suitcases in tow, I observed them strolling out the exit door and then climbing into waiting cars and taxicabs, apparently headed for their respective homes.

Standing at the second floor balcony (with my eyes looking downward), it was heartrending enough for me. But when I heard a remark made by a nearby student, my depression plunged a fathom deeper. The girl made sure I was within earshot of her statement.

Speaking in the midst of fellow classmates, she angrily said, "The reason we didn't get to go on our trip is because Mr. H stole our money!"

I looked at the begrudging young lady as she continued her stroll down the hall but I offered nothing in rebuttal. After all, she was very angry, very ill-informed and she had a great need to vent and blame someone. And, seemingly, since she esteemed, both, Ms. Cline and the principal (a white man), she felt comfortable in accusing a lowly black man (me) of bold and brazen thievery.

Racism, Sexism, Trumpism, Pseudo-Christianity and the Cinema

She, like all of her fellow choir members and peers knew nothing about my past efforts to try and avert the catastrophe. Therefore, at that specific moment, I elected to remain silent and roll with the punches (although they were all below the belt)

In the short aftermath of that doomed trek to Kansas City, Missouri, I went into a kind of reparation mode. I immediately contacted the K.C. hotel, cancelled our reservations and formally requested the return of our portion of the money sent to them. As specified in the contract, it allowed the hotel to retain one-half of the reservation fee. In addition, since the amusement park admission tickets were non-refundable, (owing to Ms. Cline) I was in possession of them also.

Therefore, in an effort to finally close out the nightmarish episode, I took the initiative to equally distribute the left-over monies to the participating students and then presented each of them a single "Worlds of Fun" ticket.

I informed them that the tickets were valid for the rest of the season and hoped they would, somehow, get to Kansas City to use them.

By the way (but not at all surprising), when I assembled the choir members together and proceeded to distribute the residual monies and the amusement park tickets to them, both, Ms. Cline and the principal were inside the selected classroom. And neither of them took any credit whatsoever for the failed venture.

In retrospect, I am pretty certain that a number of those students (especially, the ones who were in the gospel ensemble) have gone through life, recollecting me as the unscrupulous and dishonest culprit who sabotaged their out-of town trip. With the passing of a few months, I was able to forgive the school's principal for his overt gullibility and bad judgment, but since Ms. Cline, who obviously considered herself a Christian, stayed altogether silent and shouldered none of the blame for the fiasco, I still begrudge her somewhat. Since it wasn't them, I am sure many people might brand me petty and accuse me of overreaction as well, but it remains steadfast in my craw. Ms. Cline's foolhardiness managed to soil my good character and that is something I've worked diligently to keep intact. I thoroughly resent any garnishment whatsoever!

Throughout my life, I have wondered about Ms. Cline's mindset in the midst of that ill-fated trek to Kansas City, Missouri. Did she really believe that God was going to "provide" a bus and a driver on that day? I truly believe in miracles and I personally know that God helps individuals in extremely rough times, but can a person be so fanatical and brainwashed that he or she becomes oblivious to plain-old common sense? Then again, if the teacher was confident that the Supreme Being would "provide" her with an unsecured (supernatural) bus driver, void of a negotiated contract and all, then why didn't she rely on God "providing" her with everything else?

Specifically, why didn't she implore the Lord to book that K.C. hotel and purchase the Worlds of Fun tickets too? I know I sound absurd, but it would have saved a lot of wear and tear (along with mental anguish) on me. All kidding aside, Ms. Cline was the kind of so-called Christian who gives Christianity a bad name and leaves a bitter taste in one's mouth.

Lowdown, Dirty Shame

While some people make a complete mockery of religion (like my teacher associate, Ms. Cline), there are other folks who treat it like reusable, wet clay They skillfully mold it into any diverse position that bolsters and promotes their personal agendas. And when I reflect on the so-named "Evangelicals" circa the Donald Trump administration, they deftly fit the bill. They wholeheartedly back a president who has no scruples, no morals, no firm belief in righteousness and they continually give him a pass (something, they call a "mulligan") whenever he makes a misstep—which, seemingly, is daily.

Racism, Sexism, Trumpism, Pseudo-Christianity and the Cinema

They stand proud and ready to yield the Commander in Chief forgiveness, even though he, himself, does not even opt to ask for it. Apparently, the current POTUS is above that. Reportedly, the man has never asked God's forgiveness for anything!

However, the Evangelicals defend him to the very hilt. But, sadly, it's not because they're so Godly or God-fearing either. It's actually because they, like our President, catapults money and wealth above any Supreme Being. And I wish masses of people would stop lying to themselves and others, clergymen included. Because, in reality, money is more dear to them than God ever was. And that, specifically, is Trump's claim to fame. In my estimation, if the President was Catholic, he would pay someone to go to confession for him.

Am I being overly critical of the POTUS? Not really.

However, as I stated priorly, there is nothing derogatory or undeserving I can say about the man that has not already been said. He is so egotistical and self-grandiose that he's sickening.

Personally (and this is something I once said about Gov. George Wallace of Alabama), I believe he's beyond salvation. However, despite my disdain for the current president, my criticism is directed at people who should know better.

Like people in the Congress, clergymen (and especially Evangelicals) and parents who essentially shirk their role in raising upstanding and wholesome children. And when I fixate on that latter group (the lackluster parents), I wonder how many of them, even though they are staunch Trump followers, can earnestly state that they long for their child to grow up and be like our current president. They may very well be envious of Trump's wealth and the high office he holds also, but the man is barren of compassion, honesty and marked integrity and (in the deepest regions of their hearts) those parents know that that's true.

Up until the 2016 election and shortly after President Trump's inauguration, I sincerely believed that the majority of the elected officials in Washington, even the Republicans were representative of the praiseworthy qualities I alluded to above. To my personal chagrin, I actually bought into the idea that they were in public life to serve and promote the welfare of the American public.

However, when so many of them began to fold like accordions and dance to Trump's divisive tunes (the great majority of them, Caucasian), I began to see them for who they really are. While I expected a degree of partisanship, I was astounded in the wake of hypocrisy and preposterous lies; all in a collective effort to render a bizarre, erratic and obnoxious Chief Executive normal and sane.

Sorrowfully, the majority of the Republicans continue to engage in that charade, regardless of the diminished morality and declining righteousness. And to think many of them are parents themselves and how they can look their offspring in their faces is way beyond me.

But, it wouldn't surprise me one iota if the greater majority of them see themselves as Christians too. And that says a mouthful in itself. No wonder there are so many confused, disillusioned and mean-spirited youngsters populating America. Having parents who no longer ascribe to Christian principles, why should they feel hopeful and optimistic? Plainly speaking, they cannot! For they are miniature satellites of substandard parents who eagerly applaud and hail Donald J. Trump as their supreme standard-bearer. And that's an admiration I will never, ever understand.

In spite of everything I've said thus far and what ever I say from here on out, I was born an emotional child and I'll die an emotional man. Every time (not sometimes, but everytime) I see the film footage of a thin, unarmed young black man being shot down by the police in Chicago, wherein he spins around and then falls dead to the pavement, I am reduced to tears. Every time (and not periodically) I see the news footage of the older Afro-American man fleeing a white cop and being repeatedly, and calmly, shot in the back by that so-called law officer, I can't help but weep.

When I think about my empathetic and compassionate nature, I frequently reflect back to a very popular, but yesteryear

Racism, Sexism, Trumpism, Pseudo-Christianity and the Cinema

motion picture. It was entitled, "Imitation of Life." In it, the black protagonist, a woman named "Annie," poses a very relevant question to her Caucasian friend and co-protagonist (played by Lana Turner, her name was "Laura") and it resonates with me till this very day. In one memorable scene, Annie's daughter (who clearly looked white in appearance) was virtually devastated in the throes of white race hatred and Laura practically implored Annie to try and console her distraught daughter.

However, almost instantly, Annie responded with a rather poignant query of her own. She asked, "How do you tell your child that she (or he) was born to be hurt?"

Now, in reality (but in another world) black parents should not have to utter such disparaging words to a child they love and cherish. But, sometimes, we do not have much of a choice. We are compelled to tell our mentally wounded children God's truth, even though it breaks our hearts. And to my great sorrow, I believe white folks have no idea what I'm talking about. I guess it's a "black thing."

To be frank, I'm not trying to garner sympathy or even empathy from anyone. Nor do I expect people to identify with my mental anguish, and especially white citizens. It would not comfort me whatsoever. But a vexing question swirls in my mind. What exactly do individuals of the Caucasian persuasion see when they observe the news footage I previously recounted?

Over the years, I've come to the realization that a white person and a black person can peruse the very same, beauteous sunset and perceive two, entirely different things.

Therefore, when white folks envision the two shooting episodes I referenced, do they see a human, flesh and blood individual being coldly murdered? Or do they find solace in their sphere and see a rabid, mongrel-dog being gunned down?

As I've said time and time again, there is nothing that white people say or do or think that remotely surprises me. However, when it comes to those alluded to murders, if they view the two victims as less than human, do those individuals have the gall to consider themselves Christians? It may not be a real word, so it's not in Webster's dictionary or anyone else's dictionary, for that matter, but (in my estimation) those types of individuals should be identified as "hyperchrist" and they should feel shameful.

Throughout this book, I have maintained that, "Everything in this country has to do with race." And I have experienced nothing that has remotely eroded my stance. When the topic of "gun-control" is discussed, white folks take refuge in citing 'Black-On-Black' crime in the inner cities (as if 'White-On-White' crime is non-existent). When the 'Black Lives Matter' issue comes up, I've heard resentful Caucasians yell, "White Lives Matter" too (although they long to delete and replace it with more). When immigrants are referred to as "Dreamers," white factions are quick to argue that 'Americans are Dreamers' too (meaning, white dreamers).

And whenever someone criticizes Donald Trump (especially, a black critic), a demeaning remark about former President Obama is on the tip of the tongue of the average Caucasian man or woman who supports him.

Notably, many of the so-called "Evangelicals" (expressly, the white ones) are scattered throughout the ranks of Trump's steadfast and, sometimes, fanatical base also. And although they will loudly cry foul and fiercely denounce my negative assessment, their suppressed but ever-present racism and biasness trumps their rather luke warm faith time and time again.

I well know that I sound like a broken record, but I am virtually unshakable when it comes to the deeds and misdeeds of America's Caucasian populace. I am practically a scholar when it comes to the history of this nation. White folks arrogantly coined the phrase, "The end justifies the means" and they proudly own it. Unfortunately, white Evangelicals ascribe to that premise also. That, too, is not at all surprising to me either.

However, I have to admit that I am totally baffled, confused

Racism, Sexism, Trumpism, Pseudo-Christianity and the Cinema

and appalled when it comes to Afro-American Evangelicals, and particularly the ones who appear to be in agreement and total lockstep with President Donald John Trump. I ask myself, 'What the hell can they be thinking?'

Taking a prolonged and in-depth look at the POTUS, here is a man who secretly despises people who look like them (openly calling black NFL football players "sons-of-bitches"); an individual who blatantly discriminated against people of color (in the housing field); a man who advocated the incarceration and execution of innocent Afro-American suspects (the 'Central Park Five'); a person who intensely hated this country's first and only black president (the 'Birther' fiasco); a man who branded distinguished Congressional members "treasonnous" (the Black Caucus) and a President who stooped so low to label poverty-stricken, black-populated regions "shit hole countries" (referencing Haiti and assorted African provinces).

Now, I am not insinuating (or advocating) that Afro-American Evangelicals should shun or denounce our current POTUS solely due to his racist "past" or his "ever-present" rather mean-spirited vernacular. I am one hundred percent positive that I'd be subjected to one vocal platitude after the other about forgiveness and repentance, which is vital whenever Christianity is discussed.

But, I beg to differ in regards to one of the forestated premises. Donald Trump's racism is not languishing somewhere in the past and it is not even on the back burner. It is thriving and well and it is living in the man's heart. Allow me to supply you with 'food-for-thought.'

In April of 2018, when a racist white boy elected to launch a shooting attack at a Nashville, Tennessee 'Waffle House,' an Afro-American man (James Shaw Jr.) stepped up and wrestled an automatic rifle from the hands of the murderer. Mr. Shaw's heroic actions were applauded on TV and throughout the nation, that is, by everyone but our Commander-in-Chief.

Then, after several weeks passed by (and after much prodding and criticism from the American public), the POTUS telephoned Shaw to cite him for his heroism. Although the Republican 'excuse birds' were aflutter everywhere, it wasn't because the president was too busy, it wasn't because he was unaware of the happening, it wasn't even because his computer was on the blink!

Simply stated, in the true heart of Donald Trump, BLACK LIVES DO NOT MATTER. And all the "spin" in the modern world cannot alter that fact!

In May of 2018, when a murderous, evil-inspired white boy elected to launch a shooting attack at the 'Noblesville West Middle School' in the state of Indiana, a Caucasian man (teacher–Jason Seaman) stepped up to thwart the assault on behalf of his love for his students. Mr. Seaman was shot three times and, thanks to God's mercy, he survived. Almost immediately, Seaman was hailed as a real-life hero, and deservedly so. Oddly enough, the POTUS was amongst his applauders and praisers so much so that he phoned Mr. Seaman on the very next day to tell him so.

I have no idea what the forestated tells the average person (especially, if they're white and a part of the Trump's base), but, to me, it affirms something I have always known: In his heart of hearts–Donald Trump dearly believes, WHITE LIVES MATTER–MORE!

Frankly speaking, it doesn't matter much to me if black Evangelicals or pseudo-Christians love or loathe Donald John Trump. ("To thine self, be true"). But enough is enough! Speak right, think right and be right! If an individual is subject to rebuke and emerges totally unmindful of sincere repentance (in spite of his or her station in this life), then that person is not truly sorry. While Jesus died for mankind's sins, (and I'm sad to say this), it appears to me that some clergymen stand ready to lie for the President's sins and wrongdoing. Evangelicals may yield him a pass, deeming it a Mulligan, but I have, yet, to run across that term in the Holy Bible.

Most certainly, I realize that a vast number of Evangelicals and

Racism, Sexism, Trumpism, Pseudo-Christianity and the Cinema

self-declared Christians will stand ready to scold, chide and rebuke me in regards to my foregoing commentary, even the ones who look somewhat like me. They will cry foul and offer up homespun slants on my rhetoric. But at least I'm honest and sincere. I wonder if they can make a similar claim.

Epilogue

As a prelude to my lengthy commentary regarding RACISM, I made a profound and straight forward statement. I asserted that, "Until Caucasian people can bring themselves to declare (with sincerity) they would rather be right than be white, the United States of America will always be a sphere of racial hatred, unrest and violence." Personally, I believe in that hypothesis entirely, therefore, instead of harmony and reconciliation being on the horizon, nationwide strife and turmoil will remain deeply embedded and evasive. Mendacity and hypocrisy lives on and on and on.

Additionally, when I revisit that foregoing RACISM segment, I am obliged to own up to a particular oversight as well.

However, upon reflecting on that select omission, I must confess it was on purpose and not at all a momentary blunder or a mere accident on my part. Therefore, it was purely by design. All along, it was my intent to reference it when I was in the process of closing out this book. The average reader may emerge totally oblivious of the point I'm alluding to (or even scoff at my underlying meaning), but it is relevant and as crystal clear to me as that magnificent sunset that I recently spoke of. Throughout this written piece, I occasionally indicated that I had my own office when I worked at a Saint Louis public high school. But while the proceeding happening is not remotely about my tenure with the city's Board of Education, there was a sign that was affixed to my office wall (right above my desk) that was acutely relevant to it. The sign simply read, "Ignorance can be fixed–but stupid is forever."

Upon revisiting a certain episode that took place in August of 1963, when I was an enlistee in the U.S. army, I recounted my very first run-in with overt racism in the so-called 'Deep South.' I, along with three of-my soldier cohorts (one of them, a fellow black man, and the other two, white) were in downtown Augusta, Georgia, standing betwixt two movie theaters, and trying to decide upon which feature film we wanted to see.

If the reader recalls, in spite of our group being attired in dress khakis, our desire for admittance into the selected movie house was soundly dashed. The two white soldiers were welcomed but "colored peoples could not go to that show" or "the one up the road a piece neither."

That was the gist of the words that came from the mouth of the young white girl in the ticket booth, just prior to me showing my naiveté and ignorance. Without displaying any semblance of discouragement or anger, I politely asked,

"Miss, could you direct us to… the colored part of town?" Taking a moment to point to her left, the young lady stated, "Walk about a mile, or a mile and a half, maybe. You'll sooner or later come to a railroad track, and you jest about will be there. Ain't too far from here, I'd say."

Adhering to the girl's direction, the four of us embarked on the hike to the 'colored part of the town.' And once there, as I assumed the role of a knowledgeable leader, we came upon a black tavern and proceeded to enter it. Locking eyes with the nearby bartender, I casually spoke, asking, "Sir, can we trouble you for four, large bottles of beer?"

Upon looking back, I don't know what I expected that bartender to say, but I certainly wasn't ready for,

"Boy, I don't serve no white motherfuckas in here! What's the matter with you, nigga? Where you from any ways? Get 'em outta my place and take yo' black ass wid 'em!"

I, of course, was not only taken aback, I was livid and practically fighting mad!

However, before I could even mount a verbal retaliation of my own, a voice of calm and reason seemed to come out of thin

Racism, Sexism, Trumpism, Pseudo-Christianity and the Cinema

air. Although none of us (not me or my three comrades) noticed him sitting in the bar's rear, Master Sergeant Ellis Ruomo (from my assigned unit) rapidly came forward. And he was as visually incensed as the bystanding bartender was.

"PFC Harris, where the hell do you think you are?" he admonished me. "You are in the prejudice and racist deep south! What's the matter with you? The only way you four guys can stay together is: Well, you can go back to downtown Augusta–take a shuttle bus back to our camp site–or take the one that goes to Fort Gordon. Otherwise, you guys can split up. You and Williams can stay put here, I'll smooth it out with Mr. Mason over there, but the white boys, they gotta go. I'm sorry, but there's no other way."

Although his fellow Caucasian comrade opted to align himself with Sgt. Ruomo's alluded to proposal, suggesting that we separate due to race, my close-knit friend, Tony, was staunchly against the idea. Immediately, he spoke up, stating, "No matter what, I'm gonna be with Barry. If we have to go back to Greenville (South Carolina), I'm gonna be with him." Of course, since 'Barry' is my middle name, he was talking about me.

Well, as things turned out, all four of us returned to downtown Augusta, Georgia, we jumped on the shuttle bus headed for Fort Gordon, we drank beer at the post exchange (PX), dined on pizza and went to the post theatre. There, we enjoyed watching 'The Time Machine,' starring Rod Taylor. After all the anguish and mental trauma we encountered that day, it ended with serenity and joyfulness. And somewhere along the way, when I seriously replayed that happening in my mind, I realized that my ignorance had been clearly fixed. To me, it was a 'teachable moment.'

Prior to that rather depressing but eye-opening episode that transpired within the confines of that black-owned tavern in Georgia, I honestly believed that Afro-Americans who were born and reared in the deep south regions (states such as Alabama, Georgia, South Carolina and, of course, Mississippi) were collectively subservient and docile when it came to their

Caucasian oppressors. In all probability, I had seen a slew of movies that depicted black submission in those southern regions. Plus, owing to the evening news broadcasts and the media in general, I was certainly aware of Rev. Dr. Martin Luther King's ongoing "nonviolent" methods of protest. And while I wasn't entirely sold on Dr. King's techniques, I was quite familiar with them.

However, although I did not make a big deal of it, something occurred inside that bar that not only warmed my heart, it managed to lift up my sagging spirits. In spite of harnessing my hurt and anxiety in the wake of being racially ostracized at that downtown movie theatre, I was silently exhilarated in light of the declaration mouthed by my dear friend, Tony. Without hesitation, Tony said, "No matter what, I'm gonna be with Barry." And although everyone else in that tavern was unaware of my inner joy, it was a feeling of fondness I never, ever forgot.

Once again, I admit to being a life-long sentimentalist and somewhat of a romantic (or bromantic) too. I have always had an enduring and insatiable love for people in general. And I believe wholeheartedly in true friendship and close-knit camaraderie as well.

But, sometimes, I fall prey to wonder. And especially when it comes to black and white liaisons, and essentially males. When I take time to candidly assess my half-century relationship with my cherished friend, Tony, and think about the miles that separate us, along with our restrictive and periodic interactions, I have come to wonder if it's genuine or is it disingenuous?

Is it solvent or even real? Furthermore (and this is the proverbial bottom line), is it even possible or feasible to maintain and nurture an authentic black-white friendship in such a tumultuous and racially polarized country such as the United States of America?

I absolutely abhor admitting this, but I did not entertain those foregoing questions prior to the Donald Trump presidency! I was ultra-secure in my relationship with Tony and because I "love" him so, with the beautiful memories I hold so dear and our fifty-

Racism, Sexism, Trumpism, Pseudo-Christianity and the Cinema

five-year devotion to each other, I was positively certain it would last and endure forever.

Although I may have been looking through rose-colored glasses, there was a time when I viewed our friendship as 'a story for the ages,' something to celebrate and rejoice over. I don't expect anyone to comprehend or even appreciate this:

But even today, when I fondly think of Tony, or physically lay my eyes on him (as I did in 2016), I still visualize the smiling 18-year old boy I initially came to love and treasure. In reality, it was before Tony was married, prior to him fathering his first child, well before he became a San Antonio police officer and, especially, before he was, to some degree, tainted and soiled by the so-called American way.

Naturally, my prized friend would vehemently argue that he has not been tainted or soiled. But I would have to respectfully take issue with him. And I am sure, too, that he would firmly deny being racially biased, and, possibly, in the name of our lifelong comradeship. However, having one or, maybe, two Afro-American friends does not exempt a white person from being a racist or having racist tendencies. And, ironically, it sometimes emboldens their biasness. Meaning, they could be more stringent and unyielding when interacting with black folks—and solely because they have a cordial and established relationship with an Afro-American. Then, to complicate matters even further, just suppose the bias-free Caucasian happens to be a former police officer? Like my dear cohort, Tony. Sounds somewhat contrived, doesn't it?

Now, in final retrospect, if any individual took the time to read this book in it's entirety (whether they are black, brown, red, yellow or white), he or she would probably conclude that I am, as the book's author, extremely dogmatic when it comes to being just and fair-minded, compassionate and empathetic and morally upstanding and prudent. In addition, the average reader might perceive me as 'idealistic' and a 'dream merchant' as well, especially when it comes to true friendship and selfless devotion to others—and despite racial origin.

Think what you will, but I am not being haughty or patting myself on the back in regards to the following scenario. And, besides, it never really materialized. But in mid 1964, when I was still soldiering in Fort Sam Houston, Texas, my cherished friend, Tony, received orders to go to South Vietnam. At that particular time, my cohort was married, the doting dad of a beautiful baby boy and residing off-post with his family.

All of the foregoing, I took into consideration, and since we had the same job description (MOS), sported the same rank (PFC) and were in the same unit (the 250th General Hospital), I opted to volunteer in his stead. In reality, I was single, had neither 'chick' nor 'child' and my heart was very much in it. However, after playing verbal volleyball with, both, my Commanding Officer and Company Commander, I was flatly turned down. For the first and only time in my life (till this very day), I was yielded favor solely due to race.

After the C.O. tried to discourage me by informing me that I would have to extend my time in the service (I countered that I would), he affirmed his decision by telling me, "There's already an inordinate number of Negroes being sent to Southeast Asia." The one thing I could not do was to turn white. I left the headquarters building, defeated and tearful.

Throughout the writing of this book, I purposely skirted around the foregoing story. As I indicated previously, I did not want to come across as braggadocios or self-grandiose either. Plus, it was an idea that, alternately, died on the vine. However, whenever I find myself focusing on the 'Trump phenomenon' (which is way too often), that yesteryear remembrance regularly comes to mind. And not just sometimes, but all the time!

Firstly, how does a man (who was born with a silver spoon-deferment) arrive on the American scene and instantaneously be granted the power to redefine "patriotism" in pursuit of his racist

Racism, Sexism, Trumpism, Pseudo-Christianity and the Cinema

agenda? Personally, I can't imagine Donald Trump being my Commander-in-Chief.

Secondly, how can Caucasian soldiers who have served side-by-side with Afro-American comrades in various war arenas (such as Korea, Vietnam, Iraq and Afghanistan) return stateside and still be as racist and indifferent as they were priorly? Apparently, 'Brothers-in-Arms' entirely overlooks black brothers.

Thirdly, are there any Caucasian NFL players who are adamant about doing the right thing, instead of the white thing? Have any of them ever considered 'taking a knee?' In addition, how can white football players have no regards whatsoever for the plight of their longtime black teammates. Again, I guess it's singularly a black thing. But, for God's sake, it certainly ain't the right thing!

CPSIA information can be obtained
at www.ICGtesting.com
Printed in the USA
JSHW021233041122
32574JS00002B/53